This book is dedicated to:
Monkey, Tabby, 260, Samantha, Beaujolais,
Lucky, Sugar, Chi Chi, Groucho, Happy,
Bootsie, Bear, Cali, Thick Neck, Harry,
and Roxie

A special thanks to AQ

Any resemblance to actual persons,
living or dead, or events in these stories is purely coincidental.

This book contains acts of bravery and stupidity,
and should never be attempted again.

Copyright © 2023 by Robert F. Byrne
www.robertbyrne.com

ISBN: 979-8-218-29655-1

Back cover photo credit - Mike Winger

YES,
this really did happen

ROBERT F. BYRNE

MY STORIES

FOREWARD

Without a decent drummer, no band can succeed. If he doesn't swing, the band sucks. If he overplays, he ruins the show. I've played in two bands with Bob, and he swung both times, and he never overplayed. He was the solid rock on which both bands built their groove. Even more crucial, he was the soul of both outfits. While the guitarists fiddled with their tuning and their pedal boards, the bass player rolled in late, and the keyboard players worried about their presets, Bob sat quietly in the back with his arms folded, always ready to share a lighthearted story if things got a little too tense. Certainly, holding the beat and signaling the build to a chorus is crucial business for a drummer, but if he's miserab e, cantankerous or lazy, no rehearsal or gig is ever going to end well.

When the singers in those two bands got temperamental - as singers often do - Bob would smile, shift on his throne and release the tension by sharing one of his tales, and I often wondered how someone who seemed so relaxed and quiet could get into trouble so often. As this book shows, he got into an awful lot of hot water and, now that I've read it, I wonder if I ever knew Bob at all.

At the start of this volume, Bob notes, "Any resemblance to actual persons living or dead, or events in these stories is purely coincidental." Having spent many wonderful hours in dank, smelly, windowless rehearsal rooms and in clubs with stages that were even worse, I can tell you that Bob is probably lying about the 'coincidental' part and anyway, who cares? One of Bob's stories is just what you need to get you smiling again.

I have traveled the world and met scores of fabulous people, but some of my most treasured moments have been spent in a few of those horrible rehearsal rooms while Bob would tell us one of his tales, and then counted us off.

"Ready? One, two, one, two, three, four..."

Nigel Dick - Music video and film director, writer and musician

ELVIS

The ad read, "Looking for an experienced drummer for the top Elvis impersonator performing in Las Vegas. Must have impeccable timing and an exceptional attitude."

I was at another low point in my musical career and happened to read that ad in the local music newspaper.

Already in several bands and orchestras in and around the Los Angeles area, this opportunity sounded different — it would actually be a paying gig.

In my many years of working in the music industry, I always found that most musicians and singers have huge egos, which is probably the reason why they have the nerve to get up on stage in the first place.

Although not much of an Elvis fan, nor impersonators of any sort for that matter, I needed to pay my rent.

The audition was to be held at a location in Encino, an upscale neighborhood located in the San Fernando Valley.

After arriving at the house, I found the garage had been converted into a makeshift rehearsal studio, equipped with old carpet draped on the walls that smelled of stale beer, cigarettes, and twice-worn cologne.

After meeting the other musicians, I quickly set up my drums.

I guess the impersonator was too important to attend the audition, and was nowhere to be found.

The band leader ran me through five of the lesser-known songs from the Elvis catalog, and then asked me to do a three-minute drum solo.

They all agreed that I was pretty good, but then again, what's so difficult about Elvis songs?

We all grew up with them, heard them hundreds of times and, unfortunately for some of us, played them even more.

At this point, the guitarist went into the house to retrieve Elvis.

The other musicians stood at attention, like a little army waiting for their commander.

"Elvis" swaggered into the studio as if he were appearing on stage at Caesars Palace, to a packed house of adoring fans.

The room fell deathly quiet.

Sporting white oversized sunglasses, and skin-tight pants that might have burst with his first gyration, he exuded a major God's-gift-to-the-world attitude.

Apparently, any notice of who may have become the newest band member didn't interest him at all.

He sauntered over to the front of the band, took a breath and struck a pose, while slowly grabbing the fake gold-plated microphone off its stand.

I broke the silence by quipping, "You must be Elvis."

He froze, then placed the microphone back on its stand, and retreated to the house.

The guitarist quickly laid down his Les Paul and chased after him as if he was an injured puppy.

After a few minutes, the guitarist came back out, told me that my audition was over, and invited me to leave.

Evidently, they were looking for a drummer, not a comic.

AT THE SOUND OF THE TONE

At the age of 18 and still living at home, I desperately needed to bring my parents into the 20th century, so I decided to get them an answering machine.

They had already stopped answering the phone and taking messages, since most of the calls were always for me.

I would come home and hear comments like, "Just to let you know, the phone kept ringing off the hook today while you were out."

Good grief!

So, I took matters into my own hands and bought the best answering machine on the market and set it up in the kitchen.

The new gadget was all too high-tech for my parents to get involved with, but they agreed to the upgrade since it relieved them of any responsibility for relaying my messages.

In those days, outgoing messages were usually extremely boring, so I wanted to record something creative that would spark some interest and fun for the caller.

I found the perfect solution by recording as my outgoing message the audio from the last scene of my favorite classic movie, *Casablanca*.

It's the scene where Rick shoots Major Strasser dead after a verbal exchange at the airport hangar.

Right after hearing the loud shot from Rick's gun, I added, "Just leave your name and number."

It worked great, and I was even getting a lot of complimentary messages left by my friends.

A week or two later, I came home late one night and found my dad waiting up for me.

He sternly asked, "What the hell did you do?"

I immediately thought that was a trick question because it could have been any number of things.

As it turned out, earlier that night my parents had been to a party and came home to a street full of law enforcement and emergency vehicles.

They had been greeted at the front door by paramedics, as several police officers with guns drawn were going from room to room looking for the shooter or the victims.

Apparently, a friend of my Dad's had called the house earlier that evening and, not being familiar with answering machines, or the movie, *Casablanca*, he was convinced that a real shooting was taking place, and immediately called the police.

Luckily, my parents had a sense of humor and didn't shoot me, although, in my family, I was the usual suspect!

MY FIRST GIG

Who knew that at the tender age of seven, I would someday join a three-piece band that would eventually lead me on a lifelong journey and induction into the Rock & Roll Hall of Fame?

Nobody, because sadly, that never happened.

What did happen at that tender age, was that one day, on the way home from church, my mom suggested that my sister, my two older brothers and I, needed to develop some kind of musical talent.

She probably thought our lives were going nowhere at the time.

She went on and offered to pay for lessons for any musical instrument of our choosing.

Naturally, I picked drums after already being a big fan of Buddy Rich and Gene Krupa.

I watched them on all of the TV variety shows during the 1960s, and was amazed by how they led their bands and captured the audience's attention, especially during their solos.

After years of lessons, practicing faithfully, and enjoying the great experience of playing in my school's orchestra, I knew that rock 'n' roll was the way for me to go.

I happened to meet a guitarist sitting across from me in a junior high school class, and we talked about getting together and jamming.

One thing led to another, and before long, I was in a power trio featuring guitar, bass, and myself on drums.

Our band had a collection of about 20 party songs from the likes of the Rolling Stones, The Beatles, and Cream.

We sounded as good as the older musicians in the neighborhood, if you didn't mind the songs not necessarily sounding like the original recordings.

One day, we heard about a battle of the bands scheduled at an American Legion Hall located north of Los Angeles, so we decided to go for it.

We entered the contest knowing that, at the very least, it would be our first real gig, and if we didn't win, the place was so far away none of our friends would ever know about it.

I was too young to drive, so my parents were my transportation to the show.

As always, my older sister tagged along for good luck.

After an hour's drive, we arrived at the American Legion Hall.

It was besieged with hundreds of chopper motorcycles, old trucks, and low-rider cars.

I was nervous and afraid to even walk into the dilapidated building.

The air inside was barely breathable with smoke, rancid alcohol, and body odor.

There were several pool tables surrounded by players, both of which had seen better days.

I made my way to the overcrowded bar and found a short drunk man wearing a ten-gallon hat, adorned with a silver police badge, who turned out to be the promoter of the event.

He pointed me towards the band stage, then lost his balance and fell over.

Nobody seemed to care as they stepped over him to continue ordering drinks.

Outside was an open dirt yard with booths and attractions to raise money for some charitable cause that nobody ever heard of.

The most popular attraction was an old police car that you could hit with a sledgehammer for a dollar per swing.

In the intense summer heat, the standard dress code for guys was leather vests with biker patches, long pocket chains attached to their wallets, black motorcycle boots, and beers in hand, all covered in a fresh layer of dirt.

For the women, there really wasn't much to describe other than mostly skin and tattoos.

At the far end of the large dirt field was a baseball diamond with a make-shift stage for the bands, decorated with an assortment of old and new California road signs.

Being the last band to play, we felt like prisoners waiting in the gallows for our turn to die.

All the bands before us looked and sounded professional, which made us think that maybe this battle of the bands had all been a huge mistake and waste of time.

As the sun started to set, it was our turn to climb onto the stage with our amps and my small drum set.

Before we finished setting up, the crowd started walking away, like maybe we looked too young to be any good?

Since I had been working towards this moment for the past eight years, more than half my life, this was very discouraging.

We fearlessly played our first song, "Honky Tonk Women."

Slowly, the dispersed crowd began coming back and grew large enough to surround the stage.

While playing our third song, without warning, three biker chicks climbed onto the stage and started an erotic dance contest of sorts, turning the audience into wild banshees.

This led to a 'Wet T-shirt' contest, and then quickly morphed into a 'No T-shirt' contest.

I don't remember anything in my music lessons that explained this particular phenomenon.

Not only did we win first place, but the promoter paid us to play an extra hour so everyone could continue dancing.

I could see my parents and sister in their car parked behind the bandstand, laughing and shaking their heads in disbelief.

Right then and there, I became a Rock Star!

BRIEF ENCOUNTER

It was 2:00 a.m., and normally the only people on the roads were drunks, or the police looking for drunks, but tonight was different.

We were trying to navigate home in Benny's brand-new sports car after a long night of drinking and disco dancing, but seemed to be hitting every red light out there.

Benny was a great sidekick who reminded me of Ernie on the TV show, My Three Sons, because of his lack of height, thick-rimmed glasses, and the goofy questions he always asked.

Stopped at a traffic light at the corner of Topanga Canyon Blvd and Sherman Way, I happened to glance over at the car next to us.

Seated there were two girls who looked as lonely and disheveled as we were.

I motioned to the driver to roll down her window, and asked, "Excuse me, but would you lovely ladies like to join us for a late-night bite to eat?"

Who could resist such an invitation from a disco clown hanging out a car window in the middle of an intersection?

They both looked at each other, shrugged their shoulders and, with nothing to lose, reluctantly asked, "Where?"

"Over there!" as I pointed to the all-night diner that just happened to be on the other side of the street, and then signaled them to follow us.

We pulled into the parking lot, met them at the entrance door, and we all wobbled in together.

The hostess led us through the deserted restaurant to a red leatherette-covered booth where we plopped down like we had rehearsed it before, boys on one side and girls on the other.

We politely introduced ourselves, grabbed our greasy menus, and quickly decided what we were going to order.

My half-baked plan was that once we fed the girls, it would easier to convince them to come back to Benny's apartment for a few drinks.

Our food arrived within minutes while I was having a great conversation with the petite blonde across from me.

As it turned out, we had a lot in common.

We had gone to the same elementary and junior high schools, and we might have even had some classes together.

Everything was going better than expected, and now I was hoping that this might be more serious than just a one-night stand.

Suddenly, her girlfriend pushed her out of the booth and said, "Let's get out of here!"

They both immediately got up and left without even saying goodbye.

Perplexed at what had just happened, I looked over at Benny.

Mystery solved.

He had completely passed out in his plate of Turkey Surprise, and was blowing brown gravy bubbles out of the side of his mouth.

I let Bennie sleep while I continued to finish my dinner.

Sadly, my half-baked plan was now as disappointing as my half-baked meatloaf.

QUICK CHANGE ARTIST

We were blowing up everything we could find; our model cars, planes, mailboxes, and anything my sister owned.

It was just after the 4th of July weekend and, sadly, Mikey was on his last brick of Black Cat firecrackers.

So, it only made sense to bring the rest of them to our junior high school.

We first lobbed them into the bathrooms, because with all that ceramic tile they sounded like cannons going off.

One kid came running out pulling up his pants.

This is where my idle brain kicked in and I asked, "Hey, Mikey, wouldn't it be fun to throw one into the principal's office?"

With a demented grin, he said, "Now you're thinking!"

We made our way through the maze of administration offices and finally down a long corridor to the principal's office.

It was easy to find because I'd been there so many times before.

The door was locked and the lights were off.

I always wondered where principals go because they never seem to be on campus and only show up at graduations.

Mikey asked, "So, what do we do now?"

"The vice-principal's office!" I replied because he was the next in line.

We snuck our way down the hall, like an amateur bomb squad.

Arriving at the vice-principal's office, the door was slightly ajar and we could see inside.

With his legs on the windowsill, Mr. Skagen was leaning back in his chair taking a nap.

I guess this was what vice-principals do.

We stood positioned and ready, and then gave each other the nod, which meant either go big or go home.

I held the firecracker while Mikey nervously lit the fuse.

Just then, a voice yelled, "Hey, what's going on out there?"

I panicked and tossed the firecracker inside the room and ran.

Mikey went one way, I went the other.

KABOOM!

I don't know if he saw our faces, but I didn't want to look back to give him the opportunity.

I just kept running and finally ducked into my classroom, calmly strolled in, and quietly took a seat.

I quickly asked the girl sitting next to me if I could borrow for her pink sweater and big blue rimmed glasses.

Then I grabbed her book and pretended to read, as if I had been there the whole time.

Mr. Skagen burst in a few moments later.

He walked up and down the aisles in between the rows of desks, carefully inspecting each kid like they were a piece of fruit.

I was extremely out of breath, but managed to hold my chest still while he walked past me.

Small beads of sweat were dripping down the side of my face, and real panic set in when I realized the book was upside down.

Out of the corner of my eye, I could see that he had stopped at the door, took one last look around, and then left.

Wow, that was close.

I was home free, as the change of outfits seemed to do the trick.

The teacher started instructing the class, which gave me a sense of relief.

Twenty minutes later, a girl entered my classroom and handed a small note to the teacher.

The teacher looked up and announced, "Robert, you are wanted in the vice-principal's office, now!"

The whole class turned around and laughed, like they'd done so many times before.

As it turned out, Mikey was captured soon after the incident and immediately ratted me out like a traitor.

We both got suspended for three days and had to go to the local fire station, where the captain gave us an impromptu lecture on high explosives.

I never touched another firecracker, that is, until Mikey found another stash a few days later.

THE CUL-DE-SAC

While attending a friend's birthday party, Benny and I were elected to make a quick run to the nearest liquor store to restock the refreshments for all the guests, but as we walked out of the house, we discovered a mysterious car was blocking the driveway.

It was a lowered, primer gray Chevy Impala that had very small tires and chrome rims.

Inside the car were three skanky-looking dudes wearing wife-beater shirts, bizarre tattoos, and hairnets.

The last thing someone might wear if they wanted to look tough was a hairnet, but what do I know?

I asked the driver nicely to please move his car, but what I got was some kind of stare down he must have learned while watching too many B movies.

Repeating my request, the driver finally drove slowly away, clearing the driveway.

Benny pulled out.

As we passed the other car, I leaned out my window and yelled, "F-you assholes," and flipped them off.

Well, that did it.

The chase was on!

As we sped away, Benny quickly accepted his fate and started yelling that we were going to die.

We raced erratically through several neighborhoods, at three times the legal speed limit.

At one point, their car came so close to us that I was able to throw my empty beer bottle and hit it, which only helped to escalate their hostility.

Benny was in a sheer panic when his car's gas light came on.

Suddenly, he made a quick left turn into a large development of newly built homes.

We flew up the street, only to find that we ended up in a deserted cul-de-sac.

The lowriders missed the turn and went straight.

We thought our troubles were over.

Two seconds later, they had circled back around and parked their car sideways at the bottom of the street, now blocking our only escape.

They opened their trunk, pulling out a baseball bat, crowbar, and some snow chains.

We were lab rats trapped in a cage, and I deeply regretted starting the whole road rage situation.

Benny was crippled with fear, and kept affirming that we were going to die.

At this point, I tended to agree with him.

Obviously, he wasn't going to have a solution to this situation.

Out of nowhere, I came up with an insane idea and one that you would probably only see in the movies.

I didn't think it all the way through because there wasn't any time, but gave my wild instructions to Benny.

"Benny, race down the street and aim for their car. Then, at the last minute, slam on your brakes and veer over to the right side of the street close to the curb. There may be enough room to go around their car, but we can't do it going fast. Just follow my lead and do as I say. Let's go!"

"What if they throw something at our car?" he whined.

"What do you want to do, go down and apologize? They'll kill us!" I said, clarifying our fate.

"Go!" I yelled again.

We were off, shifting through gears with our bright lights on, heading straight for them like a suicide drone heading towards its destruction.

Just as we got close, I yelled, "Now!"

Benny slammed on the brakes and the car skidded sideways to a perfect stop near the curb.

The armed lowriders ran towards us, waving their weapons like wild banshees.

I felt like Captain Cook.

I immediately jumped out of the car with one hand behind my back pretending to hold something, and the other hand flashing my open wallet, displaying a shiny badge which I had bought a few months earlier for a Halloween costume.

I wasn't trying to impersonate a police officer — no, I was trying to impersonate the whole squad.

They were clearly surprised when I barked orders for them to drop their weapons and place their hands on the top of their car.

I yelled to Benny, "Call for backup!" which he pretended to do.

His car had two big CB antennas, so it actually looked like it could have been an unmarked cop car, except for being a lime green Toyota with chrome wheels.

I walked back over to Benny's car to double check if there was enough room near the curb for our escape.

I whispered to him to roll down the rear passenger window, start the engine, and hit the gas.

As Benny put it in gear, I dove through the window opening onto the back seat.

We sped off with my legs hanging out.

I looked back and saw the dumbfounded lowriders standing there like three stooges.

Right then and there, I knew that this was the start of my acting career.

OH, MY STARS

Huey was getting married this coming Saturday and, to my surprise, his so-called best man didn't even consider giving him the all-important bachelor party.

Why is he called the best man when he ignores one of his most important responsibilities?

Being the nice guy that I am, I graciously offered to host a small soiree the night before his big day.

Obviously, his future wife wasn't so keen on the idea because she knew me and my antics.

I told her not to worry, and that we were just going to have a harmless night of drinking beer and playing cards.

I initially invited only about five or six of our friends to my small apartment, but soon the word got out.

By 8:00 p.m., there were about 15 of us.

Everyone knows that a room full of guys bonding over a game of poker is extremely boring, especially when there's only one deck of cards.

In our case, that was until someone suggested we go to a strip club.

The only halfway decent strip club was located on Wilshire Blvd in Santa Monica.

Everyone jumped in their cars and drove the 40 minutes.

As we entered the club, we could see a handful of lonely husbands scattered around the large room, almost in a trance-like state.

In the center was a long runway where the girls danced to blaring music while shedding their clothes under the strobe lights.

The city code was that the ladies could strip down only so far, leaving their bikini bottoms on, which was fine because, as guys, we imagine all women naked anyways.

Our group quickly sat down and started yelling while throwing dollar bills at the strippers, like we were feeding fish to seals.

The management didn't mind how loud or obnoxious we were because we were buying drinks like sailors on shore leave.

One guy threw so much money at this one girl that she took off her red lace bra and tossed it to him.

He quickly smelled it like it was a freshly picked flower and shoved it in his opened shirt as a souvenir.

I heard that when he got home later than night, the bra fell out of his jacket in front of his girlfriend, which must have taken some clever explaining.

After about an hour of drinking and throwing cash, we were totally plastered and out of money.

Some of the guys were too drunk to drive, so I volunteered to take four in my small Datsun 200SX hatchback.

We stuffed the shortest guy into the trunk where he puked half way home, making the car ride unbearable.

I dropped everyone off at their houses, including the very soon-to-be married bachelor.

He thanked me for being his friend and organizing one of the best times of his life.

I finally made it home by around 3:00 a.m. and passed out as soon as my head hit the pillow.

The phone rang at 6:00 a.m. with a frantic woman yelling, "Where's Huey?"

I said, "What, who is this?"

She said, "Huey didn't come home last night, and no one knows where he is!"

"I dropped him off in front of his house last night around 2:00 a.m., and that's the last I saw of him."

"I need to call the police. God dammit ROBERT!" click.

At the wedding, I found out that after I dropped off Huey, he didn't want to wake everyone up by opening the front door, so he walked around to the back of the house.

He then decided to lie down on the cool grass in his backyard and take one last look at the stars as a single man.

Yep, that's where they finally found him later that morning, still sleeping.

A CHURCH SURPRISE

Every Sunday afternoon, I had this wonderful routine;
I would attend the 8:00 a.m. service at a small Catholic
church in nearby Montecito, pick up a fast food breakfast
afterwards, and then go to my office to play catch-up on last
week's work in order to prepare for the coming week.

After about four hours of work, I would walk next door to
the swanky athletic club, work out, and then relax in the
sauna or steam room.

I had recently relocated from Los Angeles to Santa Barbara
for an exciting job opportunity creating illustrations and
animation for interactive learning CD ROMS.

Being single, this was a productive way to spend my lonely
Sundays.

One of the reasons I would go to this house of worship was
to possibly meet a nice Catholic girl, or at least that was my
plan.

I always sat alone near the back of the church, just in case
there was an unexpected bolt of lightning.

Many times, this quaint mission-style church would have
several celebrities and other impressive looking people
sprinkled throughout the congregation.

After months of practicing my weekly devotion, one Sunday,
lo-and-behold, there was a new face in the crowd.

There she was, sitting in the front section of pews close to the
altar.

Halfway through the mass, she happened to turn, notice me, and smile.

It was easy to smile back.

Either my praying or how much I put into the collection basket was about to pay off.

God only knows.

From across the church, she looked quite respectable, conservatively dressed, and, hopefully, came from a very wealthy Montecito family.

It's not that she had to have money, but with all the praying, a little bonus like that wouldn't hurt.

The next Sunday morning, she sat in the middle of the church.

Over the following weeks, she moved closer and closer towards me, like a cougar stalking its prey.

She finally made it to my pew, sat down beside me, and introduced herself before the mass began.

Thank you, god!

She was even better looking up close.

With her tailored tan blazer, white blouse, and little red bow tie, she was stylish and sexy in her own sophisticated way.

Her emerald-colored eyes were something I could easily drown in.

She exuded a sensual fragrance, like that of Nordstrom's perfume section during the holidays.

We both sat like two kids, sneaking glances at one another when the other wasn't looking.

Yes, this was my fantasy coming true, the one I was praying for—a great new job in a beautiful city, and meeting someone refined and attractive to enjoy it all with.

There comes a part during a Catholic mass when the priest asks the attendees to bow their heads and pray in silence for any special concerns they may have.

Then, after a minute or two, the priest continues with the rest of the service.

Today, I closed my eyes, lowered my head, and started reciting a small prayer of thanks for my life and my new friend.

My prayer of gratitude came to an abrupt halt when, suddenly, my dream girl stood up and began yelling a rambling speech, protesting the Catholic church's stance on abortion.

Oh my god, what the hell was she doing?

Had she intentionally plotted out this protest, or was it an uncontrollable Tourette's outburst?

This wasn't exactly the venue where anyone would have expected to witness such a radical declaration, regardless of their social or political leanings.

This was the longest few minutes I ever had to agonize through while slowly sliding my body down in my seat, in the hopes of hiding from the rest of the congregation's bug-eyed, gaping-mouthed faces.

Naturally, I was so invested in my fantasy that I automatically assumed everyone was looking at both of us as a couple.

If there was any suitable time for the great rapture, this would be it.

To his credit, the priest, after being so blatantly ambushed mid-sermon, politely waited until she was done, quietly gathered himself, and then continued with the rest of the mass.

Since then, my Sunday morning plans have changed.

I still go to work and to the gym, but now I redirect my prayers towards finding a nice Jewish girl at a local deli.

THE GAME SHOW

The bride had planned for a storybook wedding reception her whole life, except today, an unexpected page was added.

Her 300-guest wedding reception was held at a swanky Beverly Hills hotel, with no expense spared on the elegant room and table decorations, or the incredible seven-course dinner that was paired with five vintage wines.

They even handed out custom watches to each of the guests, with the bride and groom's wedding date engraved on the back, just in case you forgot what you did that night.

I was hired to play drums in the 30-piece orchestra, which included some of the top musicians in Los Angeles.

We played the jazz standards during the cocktail hour, while the guests arrived and overwhelmed the bar.

Finally, the betrothed couple arrived and proceeded to make their big entrance into the grand ballroom.

Our singer asked all the guests to take their seats, so the newlyweds could perform the traditional first dance as husband and wife.

I played a big drum roll as it was announced, "For the first time anywhere, Mr. and Mrs. So-and-So!"

The smiling couple entered gracefully, and were welcomed with a standing ovation from all their friends and family.

The bride was stunning and floated in like a princess wearing the most sensual and revealing lace gown anyone could ever imagine.

The wedding dress train was at least twenty feet long and adorned with hundreds of small pink silk roses.

Her ostentatious diamond ring could be seen all the way across the huge room.

Even the waiters stopped what they were doing and stared with their mouths open.

The lights dimmed, as a distant spotlight made them glow.

The couple began their dance but, after one turn, the bride glanced at the band and did a double take.

She blurted out, "Oh my god!"

Wiggling out of her husband's embrace, she immediately ran towards our keyboard player and gave him a huge hug and kiss on the cheek.

Then all the bridesmaids, as well as her parents, jumped from their seats and ran over to join the bride on the bandstand.

All the while, the confused groom was left frozen on the empty dance floor, like Vladimir in *Waiting for Godot*.

After five minutes of hugs and kisses, the bride returned to the bewildered groom to resume the first dance.

She continued to glance back at the keyboard player throughout the duration of the first dance.

On our break, I asked the keyboardist what all the excitement was about.

He explained that he had met the bride on a popular TV dating game show, and they started going out, but he called off the relationship because all she talked about was getting married and starting a family as soon as possible.

"When did all this happen?"

"Six months ago."

The sentimental, and what turned out to be perfect, song that the bride had chosen for this once-in-a-lifetime dance was from Elvis Presley's catalog of hits, "Can't Help Falling in Love".

LAST CHANCE

The interior of the club was dark and reeking of legal and illegal smoke, alcohol, and cheap perfume, making it the perfect venue for rock 'n' roll.

It was the very night before my wedding, and I was scheduled to play a showcase at the hugely popular Madame Wong's, located in Santa Monica.

It was where some of the biggest rock legends started out.

Our band had a large fan base, and it was standing room only for this Friday night.

While waiting offstage, holding my drumstick bag, someone approached me.

She was a gorgeous and petite blonde, in tight leather jeans and matching jacket, high heels, and sporting that unmistakable 1980's spiked hair and makeup.

This stunning creature was so totally out of my league that I could barely take my eyes off her.

She stood very close to me and asked, "Are you married?"

I stammered out, "Uh, no."

Why would someone this attractive even consider talking to me, let alone ask me that question?

What made matters even worse was that tonight was my last night of being single.

Since the guys in my band were a bunch of practical jokers, I assumed they must have paid her to approach me, and I actually asked that of the guitarist as he just happened to walk by, but he said, "No."

"Oh, dear god, is this some kind of test? Why didn't you send her to me months ago?"

We continued talking while the other band played, and I discovered that she was a jazz singer-songwriter from Canada on tour in the United States, and her father was a successful record producer.

With her angelic smile and blue eyes, I could see her lips moving, but got lost in her sensual French accent.

During our conversation, it happened to slip out that I was getting married the next day, but she didn't seem to care and, for a second or two, neither did I.

Will my wedding ceremony tomorrow turn out to be that final church scene in the movie, *Four Weddings and a Funeral*, blanking out at the altar and saying the wrong word because I was only thinking of her?

It was now my band's turn to get on stage, and so I went to quickly set up my drums.

We locked eyes during the whole set, drawn together by some magical connection between two complete strangers alone in a room.

After two encores, I stepped off the stage.

She walked over, gave me a long embrace, kissed my cheek, then turned and disappeared into the crowd.

As it turned out, my wedding ceremony the next day went fine, and I said all the right words, but unfortunately, the marriage only lasted a year.

Maybe God had thrown me a last-minute life preserver that night, but I thought it was too wonderful to be true.

LOVE IS BLIND

Everyone has that one embarrassing moment they try to forget but can't and, unfortunately, this is one of them.

Back in the 1980s, I played in and managed a jazz fusion band which was very popular in and around the Los Angeles area.

It was a blend of very talented jazz and rock musicians whose combined skills created a unique style of music.

I would often book our band at local colleges and universities for their lunchtime concerts.

These were great gigs because they provided built-in audiences that were very receptive to original music.

One quiet summer afternoon around 3:00 p.m., I had an appointment with the student activity coordinator to book our band for a show at California State University Northridge.

At this time of day, most of the students had already left campus, and it was pretty much a ghost town.

I didn't know where the office was and mistakenly parked on the far side of the school, which necessitated a walk across the entire campus to get to my appointment.

The meeting was a success as the activity coordinator was very impressed with the band's recordings and marketing package, and I was then able to secure an afternoon concert for the following week.

On the long way back to my car, I found myself in the center of a large open quad area consisting of about three acres of manicured lawn, with a walkway that connected to other sections of the campus.

While walking across the open area, I noticed an attractive girl walking about thirty yards behind me.

Now and then, I continually turned around to look at her in a positive, but flirtatious, way.

She acknowledged me, but probably thought I was some kind of pervert stalking the local campuses.

This went on for about fifty yards, and I was so distracted by her that I was completely unaware of another girl walking towards me on a head-on collision course from the opposite direction.

BAM!

We both slammed our foreheads together like two empty coconuts.

The impact threw her to the pavement, breaking her dark sunglasses and tossing her books and belongings everywhere.

She instantly screamed at the top of her lungs, "Rape! Help me! Rape!"

She flailed her white cane in every direction, trying to fend off her mystery attacker.

White cane?

Yes, a white cane.

This helpless girl rolling back and forth on the pavement was blind.

She obviously knew where she was walking and most likely had covered this path hundreds of times before with no problems.

Other students probably got out of her way when they saw her coming, so it made sense for her to think that now she was going to be raped or robbed.

I attempted to apologize and help her up, but she didn't want any part of it and continued screaming!

People came running out of the nearby buildings to see what all the commotion was about.

After about twenty minutes, the now hugely gathered crowd finally got her back on her feet and on her way.

Since the whole accident was my fault, I offered to pay for her broken sunglasses, but it was to no avail.

The next week, our band played a noontime concert at that very college, and it went quite well.

After our show, that same blind girl made her way to the stage and commented that she really loved the music.

When she heard me say, "Thank you," her mouth dropped open, a look of terror came over her face, and she quickly trotted away.

Now, apparently, my voice, in addition to my face, makes women turn and run.

RANDY'S LUNCH

My redheaded, freckle-faced friend, Randy, wore the same clothes to school every day, and everyone knew this just by the smell.

His only pair of shoes were so scuffed and worn that you wouldn't believe they were once black.

He was our elementary school's "Pigpen."

Not coming from the richest of families, he did have great qualities that many kids lack, like always being in a good mood, wanting to make people laugh, and most importantly, being able to run fast.

I lived across the street from school, and usually went home for lunch, but my mom had a doctor's appointment so, today, leaving me to eat in the school's cafeteria.

I entered the crowded cafeteria, got in line, and pushed my huge metal tray along the buffet trough, past four large sweat-soaked women who meticulously portioned out the food with military precision.

The current menu consisted of artificial mashed potatoes, meat loaf surprise, creamed corn, and what appeared to be a small, under-cooked cinnamon roll saturated with a white lumpy sweet topping.

Yum!

After paying my $.65, I grabbed my loaded tray and sat down alone at a long empty table that was littered with yesterday's crumbs and stains.

For some strange reason, three girls came over and sat across from me.

They all smiled.

I immediately turned as red as my cranberry juice, and smiled back.

Randy saw this from across the cafeteria and joined us, sitting down next to me.

We were both very shy, but together as a team, maybe, we had the courage to talk to the girls intelligently.

The conversation about frogs died after two minutes, so Randy resorted to Plan B.

He slowly mixed all his food together on his plate like a witch's brew, then added his orange juice and milk to complete the concoction.

When he ate the gray, lumpy mixture, the girls started laughing and getting grossed out, which is exactly the reaction he was hoping for.

After he finished the last slurp of his experimental lunch, he proudly opened his mouth, showing the girls that it was all gone.

For some unknown reason, they were not impressed.

Two minutes later, a glaze came over Randy's eyes as they opened wider than their sockets, and his face froze.

His whole body convulsed, then stiffened up, and with a loud gut-wrenching roar, he barfed!

It wasn't an ordinary schoolboy puke.

No, this was an explosion, like an atomic fire hydrant from deep inside his throat.

Everything he had just ingested came shooting out over his teeth with every pound of force his stomach and lungs could generate.

This human cannon was blasting milk cartons, plates, and trays off the table, while splattering the girls in vomit.

They were now officially a Jackson Pollock triptych.

Everyone in the cafeteria screamed and ran for their lives!

After about ten minutes, Randy lay in a fetal position on the floor, going through spasms like he was giving birth, surrounded by several teachers and the school nurse.

I finally caught my breath from laughing so hard, but still looked forward to quietly eating my lunch at home again.

DUMBO

Unfortunately, but fortunately, I was gifted with a nickname by my fellow elementary school students that changed my life forever.

The name was "Dumbo."

It wasn't because I was gray or overweight, but because my ears stuck out just like the Disney cartoon character.

According to one smart ass, "my ears flapped in the wind."

There was no way to try to stop the whole school from calling me names, because that would just invite more teasing and attract even more attention to my problem.

Sometimes, I would cry from embarrassment; other times I would just beat up the culprit, which probably led to my above average fighting skills at a very early age, but also an above average number of detentions.

Yes, it was my problem and no one else's, and there was really nothing I could do about it, or was there?

I was wrapping my dad's birthday present and saw the answer right there in front of me.

It was clear and sticky, and, if applied just right, maybe nobody would notice it holding my ears back.

It was Scotch Magic Tape.

Right then, I decided to take matters into my own hands.

I worked with the tape for about ten or fifteen minutes until my ears finally looked fairly normal, or at least that's how they looked from the low angle of the bathroom mirror.

To be safe, I had to test it out before trying it out at school.

My older brother was lying on the floor watching cartoons, and I sat on the couch behind him and started watching too.

I don't think he even turned around when he said, "Why are you wearing that stupid tape on your ears?"

He was no help.

I was headed back to the bathroom to see if maybe the tape had slipped or fallen off and saw my mother was coming towards me holding a basket of laundry.

From at least ten feet away, she immediately asked, "What the hell is on your ears?"

She bent down and examined my makeshift solution.

I confessed to her about my painful nickname from the kids at school.

She held me for the longest minute.

I felt even worse because now she knows she has a kid named Dumbo.

Thank heavens she was smarter than other moms and could see into my future.

She did what any intelligent parent should do and took me to see a doctor.

After a two-minute examination, the doctor recommended a simple $1,200 surgery to adjust my protruding ears.

Our family didn't have that kind of money, and now I felt really terrible about trying to flatten my ears with tape.

My mom looked right into my eyes and said, "Don't worry, Dad's health insurance will cover the cost."

We found out later it didn't, but my parents cared about me enough that they considered it a small price to pay for their son to live without a lifetime of self-consciousness.

It was the start of summer vacation, and the surgery was scheduled right away.

The operation went well and I came out of the hospital with enough bandages on my head to resemble an oversized medicine ball.

After weeks of healing, summer vacation was over and it was time to go back to school.

Anxious and scared about walking into my first class, I knew someone would remember what I looked like before, and come up with another mean nickname.

To my surprise, and relief, the name Dumbo was never mentioned again.

Years later, on a trip to Disneyland with a girlfriend, we happened to walk by the Dumbo Flying Elephant ride.

This was the first time in all my visits that I had the courage to stand close to the ride, after having always avoided that particular area of the park.

My girlfriend grabbed my arm and dragged me onto the ride while saying, "Come on, it'll be fun!"

She had no idea this was a big moment in my life.

We climbed into our elephant and flew around, up and down, for three long minutes, which brought me to tears.

Today, when I see an elephant or the Disney character Dumbo, it still reminds me of how grateful I am that my parents didn't deliver that generic encouragement speech on how special I was, but instead made the situation better for everyone.

THE MOTORHOME

Mikey wanted to impress Benny and me by taking his dad's motorhome out for a quick spin around the high school campus and through the neighborhood.

How would a 15-year old driving a vehicle three times the size of a normal car, without a driver's license, or permission, impress anyone?

Mikey's dad bought this used vehicle hoping that one day he would restore it to its original condition, just like all the other fathers who buy a dream, park it in the driveway to accumulate even more rust, while bringing down the value of the homes in the neighborhood.

This obscure 1960's RV was more square than it was aerodynamic, and very content to remain parked rather than move down a highway.

The interior, with all its exposed nuts and bolts, resembled a sheet metal rocket ship command center created for a futuristic "B" movie from the 1950s.

Mikey's mom gave it the woman's touch with hand-sewn matching curtains and chair cushions re-purposed from an old bedspread.

His dad installed a wrought iron outdoor patio set by bolting it to the floor.

I went through the kitchen drawers and refrigerator and discovered that someone had failed to throw out a box of rotten fruit.

This made it almost unbearable to breathe, even after opening all the windows.

Mikey climbed into the driver's seat like a NASCAR veteran and fired up the old beast.

The engine cranked a half dozen times, sending a huge cloud of black smoke into the street, followed by three loud bangs.

The engine finally started up, and Mikey wrestled it into gear.

We began to gradually float down the street, like an ocean liner leaving dry dock on its maiden voyage.

Benny settled into the front passenger seat, while I took full advantage of the spacious interior with all its sliding windows.

We cruised to the high school and drove onto the campus front lawn, but that was a waste of time because most of the students had already gone home for the day.

Back on the street, Mikey was doing a great job of keeping the wide motorhome in the middle of the lane, shearing off only a couple of side mirrors from some parked cars.

We pulled up at a red light where a custom Model T hot rod had stalled in the intersection.

Painted on the trunk in a big red scripted font were the words, "Big Daddy."

A heavyset gentleman in white coveralls was bent over the huge chrome engine as if he were trying to fix something.

As we waited for the light to change, it seemed like a good opportunity to get rid of the smelly rotten fruit.

I picked up the soggy cardboard box, swung it backwards, and heaved the contents towards the hot rod mechanic.

Bullseye!

I yelled, "Go!"

Mikey put the pedal to the metal, lunging the motorhome through the red light.

I fell to the floor, rolling like a loose marble toward the back and almost out the rear door.

"Big Daddy" came running, flailing his fists in the air, but with little chance of catching us.

We drove through back alleys all the way home, making sure nobody was following us.

Ah, we felt safe and sound arriving at Mikey's house.

He carefully parked the motorhome in the driveway so his dad couldn't tell it had been moved, just like in the movie, *Ferris Bueller's Day Off.*

About a week later, on a quiet Sunday morning as our family was getting ready for church, the phone rang.

My dad yelled from the back bedroom, "Robert, answer the phone!"

I picked it up and said, "Hello."

"This is the Los Angeles Police Department and I need to talk to a Mr. or Mrs. Byrne regarding Robert and a motorhome."

I immediately slammed down the phone.

Oh shit!

Seconds later, the phone rang again.

I let it ring and ring, hoping it would stop.

It didn't.

My dad yelled again, "Robert, answer that goddamn phone!"

I let it ring about eight times before picking it up again and heard an authoritative voice say, "Robert, if you don't put one of your parents on the phone, we'll send a squad car over there instead!"

After my mom had a brief conversation with the officer, we drove to our local police station for questioning.

I received a lecture on the destruction of property and its penalties.

My dad was upset and embarrassed, but my mom couldn't stop laughing the whole time.

She kept saying, "I can't believe Mikey's mother is that cheap that she makes curtains out of her old bedspreads!"

THE STORM

One of the more bizarre, albeit exciting, gigs I played was at a famous, but now defunct, nightclub located in an old section of Hollywood.

During its heyday, it was a well-known hangout where many of the top musicians, comedians, and miscellaneous wannabes started out.

The interior walls were partially painted, and were adorned with thick dusty curtains that seemed to have been used in one too many silent movies.

The tables and chairs were barely usable because they were so wobbly, and had likely come from the trash of other nearby clubs that had since gone out of business.

The film noir lighting accentuated the layers of cigarette smoke, giving the room a sultry vibe.

The bar was at one end and the stage at the other, which made sense, but what didn't make sense was where the bathroom entrances were.

They were located on a second-floor balcony that hung out directly over the cave-like stage.

It was distracting, but a treat for the audience when girls in short skirts slowly climbed the stairs to use the ladies' room.

The band I played with that night was called The Storm, and our music sounded like a cross between The Doors and Nirvana.

The musicians and the lead singer were extremely talented and connected well with the audience.

We loved performing at this particular venue because the audience accepted anything act that was new and different.

Everything was going according to plan as we loaded our gear onto the tiny stage, tapped the microphones a few times, and gave a nod to the sound engineer who was also the bartender.

As the lights dimmed, the room immediately fell quiet with anticipation.

"L.A., are you ready?" was announced loudly over the sound system.

"Headlining again, please welcome THE STORM!"

The audience applauded.

As the stage lights flipped on, a thunderous guitar chord launched us into our first song.

At that exact moment, an unexpected flow of water came spilling down from the second-story balcony, cascading out over the stage and into the audience

It was like a warm summer rain had fallen onto the front row of patrons, as they held up their drinks and toasted the band because they now felt like part of the show.

Unfortunately, it was the water from a clogged toilet in the ladies' restroom, which continued to overflow throughout our first song.

Although that night turned out to be one of The Storm's best shows, thanks, in part, to the special effects, we knew we would never receive any requests for a repeat performance

MORE FLUID, PLEASE

Kenny, Tony and I decided to celebrate the end of our high school summer vacation by going camping at the picturesque Cachuma Lake in the mountains above Santa Barbara?

We loaded up Tony's old primer-gray sedan with gear, food, and our favorite 8-track tapes for the three-day adventure.

It was a scenic drive north along the beautiful California coast and then up the winding two-lane Highway 154 toward the campground.

After unpacking and setting up our tents, we rented a small boat and loaded it with beer and fishing poles in search of tonight's dinner.

After a boring day floating in the sun, we realized that it was just the bugs that were biting.

The only thing we caught was a terrible sunburn and a headache from all that heat.

Hungry and tired, we stopped at the campground's market, bought three of their best-looking rainbow trout, hung them on a big hook, and strutted back to camp so people would think we caught them ourselves.

We placed the fish in our specially improvised beer and Tabasco sauce marinade, and poached it over the open campfire.

The taste was a bit funky, but to our delight, the noxious smell kept the insects away.

Drinking beer around an open fire with the ceiling of stars above us was a surprisingly serene end to our day.

Although, the sounds of passing cars from the nearby highway did bring us back to reality now and then.

I could never figure out why anyone would build a campground right next to a busy highway, and think it was a good idea.

Tony was wearing his old construction boots, and resting them on top of the large rocks surrounding the campfire.

"Hey, can you feel the heat of the fire through your boots?" I asked.

"Nuh, these are heavy duty, plus they're caked with mud."

Just to be funny, I picked up a nearby can of lighter fluid and squirted a small amount on his boots.

A flame shot up about a foot high.

"Can you feel the heat now?"

"No!" as he made his boots dance like the ones in the dinner roll scene in Charlie Chaplin's movie, *The Gold Rush*.

The short burst of flame only lasted a few seconds, so no real harm was done.

Never content with going halfway, I squirted a second blast on his boots.

This time, the fire shot up about two feet, like the Wizard's burst of flames in the movie, *The Wizard of Oz*.

I then decided to go for broke, and really spray his boots, but, in doing do, I accidentally drenched his socks all the way up his pant leg.

Well, that did it!

The flames exploded about four feet high, burning the insides of his Levi's.

He now looked like the movie, *The Towering Inferno*.

We camped too far from the lake for him to make a run for the water, so Kenny and I started kicking and throwing dirt on him, which only made things worse.

Suddenly, Tony came up with a last-ditch effort and unbuckled his pants, pulled them down over his boots, and tore off his shirt, blanketing what flames were still smoldering.

About a dozen nearby campers came running to see what all the yelling and commotion was about.

They saw a sight they will never forget.

Through a huge cloud of dirt and smoke, there were three drunks standing around a fire pit, with one completely naked with his clothes down around his ankles.

Yes, a perfect ending to a perfect summer vacation.

THE STING-RAY

"Faster, go faster!" I yelled, while straddling the handlebars of Mikey's brand-new blue Sting-Ray bicycle.

This bike was legendary around the neighborhoods during the 1960s, as only the rich kids owned them.

It was equipped with two rear-view mirrors, chrome fenders, a banana seat, and a slick back tire.

I navigated our course through the construction site while Mikey provided all the muscle for the pedaling.

We were going up and down the dirt hills like desperate motocross riders on the final lap of a championship race.

I now directed us towards the largest mound in the vacant field.

It must have been at least six feet high of what appeared to be hard-packed dirt.

I gave Mikey orders to give it all he's got so we would have enough speed and momentum to reach the summit.

He was behind me, grunting like a wild boar.

We hit the base of the mound at about 15 miles an hour, and flew easily up the incline.

Almost at the top, I could now see what was on the other side.

Nothing.

It looked like somebody sliced the hill in half, like a miniature Yosemite's Half Dome.

I perceived our impending doom and quickly jumped off before we got to the top.

There wasn't enough time to warn Mikey, so, unfortunately, he wasn't so lucky.

He took flight like Evel Knievel attempting a world record, and then did a nosedive straight down into a pile of old bricks and construction materials.

I was OK, but Mikey was now in a fetal position holding his right knee and screaming.

We always liked to joke around and do crazy things, so I assumed he was faking that he got hurt.

"Come on, quit it Mikey. Let's go. Now get up!"

He screamed even louder.

"Stop it. Joke's over, I'm leaving you here."

I wasn't about to play into his shenanigans, and slowly walked away.

Hiding around the corner of a nearby house, I peered back at him for about five whole minutes.

By this time, he was screaming and throwing dirt into the air, hoping to get anyone's attention.

Frustrated at this point, I decided to go tell his parents and let them be the butt of his little joke.

I took my time, casually walking to his parents' house which was half a block away.

After knocking on their front door, Mikey's mom appeared and I told her that Mikey was hurt in the nearly field, and pointed in the direction of the crash site.

Hi mom heard Mikey screaming and she took off running.

Minutes later, back home sitting in my bedroom, I could hear an ambulance racing up the street.

The next day, after Mikey came home from the hospital, I found out that in addition to the multiple cuts and bruises, he also suffered a shattered kneecap, two sprained wrists, and a several cracked ribs.

I learned two valuable lessons that day:

1. Never take a backseat in life.

2. Give your best friend the benefit of the doubt when he's screaming in an empty field.

THE MASSAGE PARLOR

An old friend whom I hadn't heard from since high school called and said he was desperate to get out of the house tonight.

He didn't say why, but I had met his girlfriend and I figured somehow she played a major role in his plea.

I suggested we go to hear a well-known band at the Whisky a Go Go, because it would be a perfect excuse for him.

The band was boring, but just watching my friend try unsuccessfully to pick up on every girl in the club was entertaining in itself.

After the show, we decided to call it a night and head home.

However, as we were leaving the Hollywood area, we saw a large sign for a massage parlor near the corner of Sunset and something or other.

Neither of us had ever been in a brothel, bordello, or any other den of iniquity before, and so I mentioned, "It couldn't hurt to at least check it out."

Since my friend struck out at the Whisky, he was more than up for the adventure.

We parked in the small dirt lot behind the establishment, took some big breaths and walked towards the front door, stepping over hundreds of cigarette butts, beer cans and what appeared to be used condoms.

I heaved open the heavy metal door, and we entered.

It felt like we were magically transported into a psychedelic dream sequence from a 1960s low budget hippie movie.

If the brick walls were painted at all, they were dark crimson with vertical lavender stripes, while other sections were covered in fluorescent yellow flocked wallpaper that ran in all directions.

The air in the smoke-filled lobby was mixed with the stench of rancid baby oil, cheap perfume and God knows what else.

A seven-foot-plus security guard with a short military haircut immediately confronted us with folded arms that displayed a tattoo of McDonald's golden arches, which I could only assume was done on a night of poor judgment.

"Sasquatch" probably got kicked out of the army because they couldn't find a uniform large enough.

He gave us a friendly grin, displaying gold bridgework which made me feel that we were the "special" on tonight's menu.

He was followed by an elderly woman who waddled over, wearing a bib shirt soiled with last week's food stains.

In a deep smoky growl, she asked, "What's your pleasure?"

A little taken aback, I found that the word 'pleasure' would be a bit of a stretch for anything this establishment offered.

I checked my wallet and then explained our situation.

"We only have sixty dollars between us. What would you suggest?"

With a disappointed glare, she responded, "You each can get a 20-minute massage with a lady of your choice."

That was the cue for two women to emerge through a multi-colored, plastic beaded curtain that separated the front lobby from the work stables.

The first to walk over was a tall, heavy-set brunette with body parts coming out of what appeared to be a pantsuit of torn denim repaired with strips of black lingerie.

It wasn't what her outfit covered, but what it didn't cover that made me feel uncomfortable.

She smiled, exhibiting a poorly-healed broken jaw injury, and winked at my friend.

The other babe was petite with a sweet smile and a long flowing blonde wig that tried its best to cover her acne scars.

She knew she would be chosen first, which I quickly did without consulting my friend.

Taking my hand, she led me through a catacomb of hallways and half-constructed rooms that were separated by paper-thin plywood.

She kept smiling back at me with her grammar school innocence.

Each room was open to the airspace above where you could hear everything going on in the other cubicles; some good, some sounded painful.

We arrived at our cubicle which measured about eight by eight feet, just enough for a ragged massage bed next to an tiny table holding a red lava lamp and an over-filled ashtray.

There were also about a dozen flower arrangements scattered around the room she apparently had earned from repeat customers.

I inspected the massage table for any fresh stains or crawling bugs, and then took my own advice and kept my clothes on.

Lying on my stomach, she immediately started massaging my neck.

After about five minutes, my curiosity got the best of me and bashfully asked, "Do you just do massages, or do you do more?"

She quickly grabbed my wallet from my pants like an expert pickpocket.

At first, I thought she was trying to rob me, but she just wanted to see if I was a cop.

She smiled and said, "Sure, but that would cost extra."

"I don't have any more cash."

She responded, "That's OK, I take credit cards."

The last thing I wanted to see on my credit card statement was a charge from a massage parlor.

What if she overcharged me, who would I call?

I could just imagine contacting my credit card company to file a claim, and having to describe the nature of the dispute.

After a frustrating twenty-minute massage, while hinting around about getting something for free, we said our goodbyes.

I headed for the front door for a breath of badly needed fresh air and found my friend passed out and slumped on a sofa by the front entrance.

I got him to his feet and helped him out the door.

As we walked across the parking lot, three police cars suddenly pulled in and parked near the front door.

Six officers wearing tactical gear jumped out and lined up in single file rushing towards the entrance.

Not wanting to find out what their mission was, we quickly got in my car and luckily sped away without them noticing us.

Halfway home, my gas gauge light came on and I needed to find a gas station.

I did, and as I was filling my tank, my friend caught a glimpse of a scantily dressed woman standing outside a sleazy hotel.

In seconds, he sprung out of my car and ran across the street to meet her.

I drove by and yelled, "Do you want me to wait?"

He waved me on.

I never found out how his night ended, but I know his relationship did a few years later.

THANKSGIVING DINNER

It was quite a surprise when my new girlfriend of only two short weeks invited me over to her parents' house for their traditional Thanksgiving Dinner and to meet her family and friends.

This angelic creature was so stunning that when they handed out good looks, someone forgot to say stop, as she received way more than her share.

If they ever made a chalk outline of her body at a crime scene, it would be festival-ready.

Her finest quality was that she was never without a smile.

With all that said, why in God's name did she want to date me?

Arriving at her house and walking towards the front door, I looked through a large bay window and saw about a dozen people drinking, laughing, and singing around a piano near a huge fireplace.

A regular Norman Rockwell scene.

The holiday aroma of home cooking and perfume filled the front yard.

After knocking a few times, I waiting patiently, a stunning, middle-aged woman appeared.

"Ah, you must be Robert."

She looked me up and down, as if she was sizing up the enemy for the first time.

A nervous chill came over me, like the moment I notice the blue and red lights flashing in my rear view mirror.

"I'm Karen's mother," she declared.

I handed her a small bouquet of holiday flowers, thinking this would impress her until I noticed the price tag was still on the cellophane wrapper.

She politely accepted them and said, "Thank you, Robert, please go upstairs and tell Karen to come down. Dinner is ready."

I entered the oversized foyer and ascended the wood curved staircase to the second floor.

Navigating down a lengthy hallway, passing a dozen rooms, I finally found Karen's bedroom.

She was seated at a large vanity, brushing her long brown hair in the mirror.

The room was impeccably designed, as for a Disney princess.

She greeted me with a big kiss, then shut the door and pulled me close.

In a whisper, she said, "I talked to my parents about your insisting that we start having sex, and they got really upset. They didn't have sex until they were married, and they expect us to do the same."

Oh my God!

I was really surprised and taken aback because I didn't know you could even have such a conversation with your parents unless you were already pregnant or had a venereal disease.

"We should save this discussion for later. Your mother said dinner is ready," I said.

We entered the dining room and found that everyone was already seated at a very long table waiting for us.

Unfortunately, the only two empty seats happened to be directly across from her mom and dad.

I bravely sat down.

Her father stood sharpening a long carving knife, and was ready to slice up the turkey, when he abruptly stopped.

The room went quiet.

He looked directly through me and, with an ominous stare, asked, "Robert, would you like to say a prayer first?"

Little did he know that my praying started before I even walked into the room!

FORE!

Today I learned a lot about my dad, and so did four other unsuspecting golfers.

After my dad retired from working at a prestigious aerospace company, we grew closer through the game of golf, as we played at his private country club at least three times a week.

I would pick him up at 5:30 a.m., and he would be dressed and ready to go at the front door.

He would always have a warm breakfast and hot coffee waiting for me to enjoy on the drive to the course.

We loved being the first golfers out there because that way we never had to wait for any slow players in front of us.

It felt like we owned our own golf course.

We kept score, but we mostly enjoyed just getting outside and spending time together.

My dad never had much to say, but when he did, it was always something interesting or funny.

He never sugar-coated his criticisms, or hid what he liked or disliked, nor did he blab out useless information or embellish facts to make him sound superior.

He once gave a lecture to a half-asleep audience of about three hundred people at the Los Angeles Convention Center, and when he began, everyone in the audience immediately sat up and began taking notes.

After his hour-long presentation, he conducted a lively question-and-answer period for almost another hour, impressing everyone.

But today was about golf, and having a great time together.

On the fifth hole, I shot away to the middle of the fairway with a perfect view of the green.

Unfortunately, my dad sliced his ball into a very heavily wooded area to the right of the fairway.

As we walked down, my dad veered off into the dense rough to retrieve his ball.

Usually, it only takes a few minutes to find a white golf ball, but he was taking a little longer than usual.

A group of golfers behind us yelled out to ask if they could play through, so I waved them on.

They proceeded to hit away, and their balls landed in the center of the fairway, near me.

My dad still had not returned.

"Hey, what happened to your partner?" asked one of the golfers.

"He's my dad, and he should be out soon," I replied.

"How old is he? Shouldn't you be worried about him?" another golfer asked.

"No, just play through."

The other golfers looked at each and decided to take matters into their own hands and headed toward the trees.

What the hell, I decided to follow the search party.

We all converged upon the primordial forest, and witnessed a sight we'll never forget.

Behind a big tree, in knee-high grass, was my dad pinching a loaf.

No wonder he was taking so long — nature called.

We all turned and quickly ran back to the fairway, hoping he hadn't seen us.

The foursome, now embarrassed, continued to play on with their game.

Two minutes later, my dad emerged holding up his ball like the golden Easter egg, and with a big smile said, "Found it!"

As they say, "When you gotta go, you gotta go!"

CELEBRATION

Tonight, I had a gig with a band that specialized in playing Bar Mitzvahs, Bat Mitzvahs and Jewish weddings.

All the members of the band were Jewish except for me, so they sympathetically nicknamed me Bob Bernstein, which I graciously accepted.

They had the shtick down, from traditional Jewish songs and candle lighting ceremonies, to the iconic child and grandmother's dance and the beloved song "Sunrise, Sunset."

They were the kings of the "chopped liver circuit."

After most Bar Mitzvah services at a synagogue, there is usually a celebration with all the guests in a large hall, restaurant or hotel banquet room.

This is where the very important "candle lighting ceremony" is held.

The custom is significant because it is a show of appreciation for those who are close to the family and have been especially important in the child's life.

Simply explained, the boy or girl stands in front of a row of unlit candles, and asks those certain individuals to join him or her while the band plays a song specifically to honor that particular person.

As an example, a very typical song for an older brother would be the theme from the movie, *Rocky*; maybe for a sister it would be "Dancing Queen," and for an uncle, "If I Were a Rich Man."

The songs are chosen well in advance so the band has significant time to learn them.

The child then reads a short poem or script about how special that person is, and together they light a candle.

The first candle usually starts with school friends, followed by aunts, uncles, grandparents, brothers, sisters and, lastly, the parents.

At this night's Bar Mitzvah party, just minutes before the candle lighting ceremony was to begin, the parents came over to our band and requested to switch out a song in the lineup, so we just randomly replaced it with another popular song for the other candle.

The ceremony began, and the room went quiet.

Everything was going according to plan until it came to candle number five, Aunt Sophia's.

The boy stopped, and in tears he announced, "My Aunt Sophia died last night, so I will be lighting the candle for her."

The guests were caught off guard and many began to cry.

Somberly, the boy turned, and started to light Aunt Sophia's candle.

Unfortunately, the band wasn't paying very close attention to the ceremony, or what the child had just said, and proceeded to play the popular replacement song on the list—the upbeat disco song by Kool and the Gang, "Celebration."

Oy!

ADJUSTING THE CLOCKS

An excellent place to see and hear jazz back in the 1980s was a nightclub located on Ventura Boulevard in Encino, California, where a popular saxophonist would host the top musicians in the world to sit in and play.

The best part of this late-night jazz scene was that there was no cover charge, which meant I would have a lot more money to spend on drinks.

As a musician myself, I would patronize this club at every opportunity because it was such a valuable learning experience to watch and listen to these talented players up close.

On one such occasion, while wearing my beer goggles at around 1:00 a.m., I noticed an absolutely gorgeous gal sitting alone at the other end of the bar looking as lonely as a hotel bible.

I was never so shallow as to judge anyone based solely on their looks, but on a scale of one to ten, she was a 12, and with her tight red jeans and snow-white smile complementing her flawless complexion, an easy 15.

Having already consumed a number of drinks, and way out of my league, I found the courage to approach her and slur out my best pickup lines.

She undoubtedly could see that I was two sheets to the wind but indulged me with small talk, probably just to get a free drink, which worked.

In our short but to the point conversation, I asked, "Would you like to go to dinner sometime soon?"

She thought about it for a second or two, took a sip of her drink as if to wash down my proposal, and returned, "How about going to the beach tomorrow?"

OMG, what could be better?

Now I can see her half-naked body before spending any money on dinner.

"Sounds perfect. I'll pick you up at 9:00 a.m."

As we quickly finished our drinks, she gave me her address, said our goodbyes, and left separately just before the management kicked us out.

The next morning, I washed my car, filled up the gas tank, and bought her some flowers just to make sure it was a perfect first date.

I arrived at her address and parked out front.

Although her apartment building was adorned with wrought iron bars on all the windows and doors, and the hallways were tagged with graffiti, I remained positive.

Her doorbell button was dangling at the end of a loose wire, so I knocked instead.

The door slowly opened, and the beast emerged, along with a powerful stench emanating from inside her apartment.

The overly ripe aroma was that of a bathroom at a highway rest stop after a long holiday weekend.

Because of my asthma, I was hoping she wouldn't invite me in, and, luckily, she didn't.

She was certainly not what I remembered from the night before, and I fought the urge to take off running.

That would be a coward's way out.

This creature's tattered beach attire looked as if it rarely, or had ever, seen the inside of a washing machine.

How could last night's tight red designer jeans dare hang in the same closet as these second-hand, ragged cut-offs?

With absolutely no makeup, or eyebrows, and framed by greasy straggly hair, her face proved to be a lot older than it had looked last night.

Yes, she had long shapely legs but, regrettably, they were well protected by an abundance of black hairs.

We exchanged pleasantries and made small talk as we walked to my car.

I politely opened the door for her, and while walking around the back of the car towards the driver's side, I swore then and there to never drink again.

She insisted we go to her favorite beach, which, unfortunately, was also where all my friends hung out.

The last thing I wanted was for any of my friends to see me with her.

Our conversation was made painfully more difficult by her one-word responses.

Within an hour, we arrived at the coast and made our way down to the sand, looking for a nice spot to spend the afternoon.

She led me around in circles, like a cat in a large litter box.

As I followed her, I kept looking around to see if I recognized anyone there.

She finally laid down her food-stained bath towel and asked, "Do you mind if I take a quick nap? I'm really tired from last night."

"No problem."

Well, at least I don't have to talk to her now.

Within minutes, her snoring was so loud that nearby beachgoers were pointing and laughing.

This was obviously the date from hell, but suddenly I got a brilliant idea!

I went back up to the car, turned the dashboard clock ahead three hours, and then did the same to my wristwatch.

I quickly returned to our spot, laid down, and then waited about 15 minutes before nudging her to wake up.

"Oh my gosh, I must have fallen asleep too, but it's 3:00 p.m., and I've got to get to work. We have to go!"

She was very groggy and disoriented, but agreed to leave.

During the drive home, I kept the radio turned off just in case the actual time was announced.

When we got back to her apartment, she smiled and said, "You seem like a really nice buy. Maybe we should have dinner."

"Sure, that would be great," I lied.

I can just imagine how confused she must have been to discover that we had gone to the future and then back in time, all on the same date.

LUNCH BREAK

It was another typical lunchtime break in the factory, where about 20 of us sat around a large picnic table, eating and enjoying each other's conversations.

My co-workers came in all shapes, colors, sizes, nationalities, religions, and backgrounds.

This cornucopia of cultures made for a wide range of adamant opinions and ridiculous arguments on a variety of inane topics.

One afternoon, Alan, the janitor, parked his utility supply cart near our lunch table and went to take his daily two-hour nap.

His cart was fully stocked with brand new supplies, which included toilet paper, hand soap, cleansers, brushes, etc.

Everything to clean the factory bathrooms and make them more inviting and sanitary than some of the restaurants I've patronized.

I happened to notice some brand-new urinal cakes on the cart and thought, women usually don't go into men's bathrooms, maybe they have no idea what they are?

I grabbed one of the fluorescent pink cakes, showed it to the woman sitting next to me, and asked, "Have you ever seen one of these?"

"No," she replied. "What is it?"

"Smell it."

She grabbed it from my hand, held it up to her nose and declared, "This smells really good."

Before I had a chance to tell her what it was, she had quickly passed it around the table to all the other women.

They each gave it the smell test, like mothers do with newborns.

Finally, one woman asked again, "Come on, Robert, what is it?"

"It's a urinal cake. It's placed in the men's urinal to cut down on the odor."

She violently threw the cake across the table, hitting my forehead and almost taking out my left eye.

Then, in unison, all the women got up and trotted off to the bathroom, holding out their hands in front of them, as if they had just touched some Kryptonite.

And so ended the instructional part of the lunch break.

THE NORTHRIDGE EARTHQUAKE

The night before the legendary Northridge earthquake,
I contemplated going to the market for my weekly food
shopping, but for some reason decided not to.

I was living in a charming 25-unit apartment complex in
Reseda, California, which resembled the set of the popular
TV show, *Melrose Place*.

This two-story complex had a large pool in the center
courtyard surrounded by lush landscaping.

My one-bedroom apartment was located on the second level,
with tenant parking spaces directly below.

The Northridge earthquake struck at 4:30 a.m. on January 17,
1994.

At first, it sounded like someone stomping up and down on
the roof above me, but when my bed started bouncing off
the floor I knew it was an earthquake.

I raced towards the front door, losing my balance and falling
several times from the violent shaking, but finally reached it
by crawling on my hands and knees.

There were several extra locks on my front door, which now
were taking an eternity to open.

While the world was shaking, I was going to die right there
trying to unlock the damn door!

The best way to describe the earthquake is to say that it felt
like bouncing down two flights of stairs in a little red wagon
while holding on for dear life.

Stepping out onto the second story landing, I was instantly drenched in water.

It wasn't rain, but the water from the swimming pool which had splashed so high that it reached the rooftop of the building and was now pouring down in waves.

There was a total power outage as far as the eye could see, and for once, it was dark enough to see the stars over the San Fernando Valley.

Tenants were going door to door and checking on each other to make sure everyone was safe.

My adrenaline was pumping, as I was now in survival mode.

Even though the building was still shaking, I rushed back upstairs to look for my two cats.

All the shelving and contents of my living room bookcases had been thrown to the floor.

My computer and TV had tumbled off their tables and were now in pieces.

I scoured my apartment, but couldn't find my cats.

I ran outside to see if they might have escaped during all the commotion, but after 20 minutes, returned to my apartment feeling emotionally drained.

Once inside my front door, I heard a faint sound coming from the hall closet.

There, under a huge pile of clothes, were my two scared cats snuggled together as close as could be.

Even though it seemed like the world was upside down, just finding the two loves of my life made everything okay.

Next came the recurring aftershocks, like endless ripples in a large pond.

Although their magnitude and frequency were predictably smaller, they kept coming.

As scary as it was being inside a building during an earthquake, it was even more frightening being outside because what you once thought was unmovable was now in motion; telephone poles, trees, sidewalks, and even mountains.

Many of the apartment buildings in my area had collapsed, burying the first floors completely.

I tried to contact friends and family to see how they were, but all the phones and power lines were down, and the streets were clogged with people and emergency crews.

My neighbor, Dan, from across the hall came over and said, "Hey Bob, I'm leaving to go down the street to check on my parents. Keep an eye on my place, OK?"

"No problem."

I started to clean up my apartment, but really needed something to calm me down.

I needed a drink.

Why didn't I go shopping last night?

Completely out of any kind of alcohol, it occurred to me that maybe my neighbor had some, so I decided to just peek inside his apartment while he was gone.

It was in shambles!

Dan was an avid antique collector and now his place was just a five-foot high heap of broken furniture, cracked Tiffany glass, punctured paintings and shattered Lladro.

After some hesitation, I warily scaled the carnage until reaching his refrigerator.

It was completely empty but, behind me on the sink was an unopened Jack Daniels Christmas gift set consisting of a bottle and two matching shot glasses.

Eureka!

I grabbed just the bottle out of the gift box and rushed back to my apartment.

Just as I was about to open it and down a big swig, a voice said, "Hey, Bob!"

It wasn't the voice in my head.

It was Dan.

I slowly turned while hiding the bottle behind me, and asked calmly, "What's up?"

"My parents were fine. I'm just going to start cleaning up my place."

When he turned and went inside his apartment, his door was left open.

I'm sure he will know the bottle is missing sooner or later.

How can I get it back in the gift box with the two glasses intact?

My only solution was to discreetly roll the bottle inside his doorway under the fallen living room curtains, and go back to cleaning up my apartment.

About an hour later, there was a loud pounding on my door.

There stood my neighbor, holding the bottle of Jack Daniels.

He held it up and said, "Dude, you're never going to believe this. This bottle flew all the way from my kitchen to the front door, but the two shot glasses are still on the counter!"

I said, "Wow, that's incredible. Let's open it!"

And we did.

I never told him the whole story, but I bet he's told his amazing version many times since.

LAKE TAHOE

It was looking like it would be another uneventful Thanksgiving weekend until Tony's dad suggested that we spend the four days at their family's cabin located in picturesque Lake Tahoe.

The reason being was that the cabin needed its annual maintenance; oiling the siding, debugging the interior, landscaping clean-up, etc.

Being only 17 at the time, I thought it would be a great opportunity to be outdoors doing what manly men do.

We loaded up his dad's truck, drove the nine hours, and finally arrived at the cabin just before nightfall.

I had imagined their cabin would be something rustic like what Abraham Lincoln grew up in, but instead, found it to be a three-story, six-bedroom chalet.

I also found out we were not alone.

Tony's dad had also invited three married couples from his Baptist church to join us for the weekend.

Nothing against Baptists, but had I known it wasn't going to be a guy's weekend, I probably would not have come along.

The itinerary included a Thanksgiving Day lunch at one of the major hotels.

Apparently, everyone else in Tahoe had the exact same idea.

There, in the hotel's large banquet room was a sizable herd of guests waiting in line for the holiday buffet.

Most of them with their mouths hanging open as if they hadn't eaten in weeks.

Unfortunately, there were the 'pickers' who had to sample every dish as they made their way along the trough of culinary delights, while everyone behind them waited impatiently.

We heard comments like, "Move your ass," "Just put the crap on your plate," and "Hurry up!"

Tony quickly asked his dad if he and I could just get lunch elsewhere.

He said it would be OK, as long we made it back to the hotel's entrance by 6:00 p.m., so we could get a ride back to the cabin.

We immediately left and found a hamburger joint two doors down.

It took us about five minutes to inhale our meals, and now had three hours to kill.

We bought a bag of sunflower seeds and sat in front of a liquor store, spitting out the shells into the street while watching the traffic go by.

We were only there for a few minutes when two girls pulled up in their small yellow Toyota.

One of the girls leaned out the window and asked, "Are you old enough to buy us some beer?"

Without hesitation, Tony answered, "Yes, but only if we can drink it with you."

That's what I liked about Tony, he was always thinking.

He walked over to the girls' car, took their cash, went inside, and came out with a 12-pack of beer and, unexpectedly, a small bottle of Jack Daniels.

Yes, he was thinking again.

We climbed into the backseat of their compact, and they drove us to their nearby campsite.

There is just something about girls in Pendleton shirts and tight blue jeans tucked into cowboy boots that makes a guy feel great about being young.

We were all getting along nicely at the campsite, and, as the sun began to set, the girls suggested we should just spend the night and continue to party.

Tony and I thought we just hit the jackpot, but, remembering being told about getting back by 6:00 p.m., we told the girls we had to go back to the hotel first to ask Tony's dad's permission.

Since there were no cell phones back then, we all jumped back into the car and headed to the hotel.

With the car's radio blaring, we pulled up and saw the Baptist group waiting outside with long faces, and arms folded in disapproval.

Tony ran up to his now totally embarrassed dad, and after a short conversation, ran back to the car.

With the biggest smile, he shouted, "Let's go!"

On the way back to the girls' campsite, we stopped at the same liquor store to buy food and more beer for the night.

Tonight's Thanksgiving dinner consisted of barbecued baloney and cheese sandwiches with a side of outdated potato salad.

After our meal, Tony paired up with the shy brunette and went off to a tent near the water to talk about nature, or something.

I retreated to the car for more privacy with my new friend.

During our make-out session, she confessed that she was on her two-week bachelorette party, and that I would just be another notch on her premarital gun belt.

At this point, it didn't bother me how faithful she was because I wasn't the one marrying her.

Rounding second base and heading to third, there was a loud pounding on the car's roof.

I immediately thought that it must be her fiancé, and that I was a dead man.

It wasn't.

It was worse.

There stood Tony, covered with what appeared to be fresh vomit.

He looked like a slime creature from a low-budget horror film.

Evidently, during their make-out session, his date lost her cookies and Tony was directly in the line of fire.

At this point, it started to rain and they both wanted to get back into the car because their tent had collapsed and filled with water.

With four people in this small car, it reeked like the mother of all stink lockers and the air was beyond noxious to breathe.

We suffered all night.

As the morning sun broke through the tall trees, we still had a half-empty bottle of Jack Daniels, and so we had a few more shots for breakfast.

Even though the night didn't go as hoped, everyone was in a great mood and sang old rock tunes on the drive back to the cabin.

When we pulled up, we could see someone's face glaring out at us from every window of the cabin; the women with pink hair curlers, the men in their lumberjack pajamas.

Again, their arms were folded in disapproval.

We said our goodbyes to the girls and walked up to the side door, where Tony's dad stood waiting for us.

We knew right then we were in deep shit when he yelled loud enough for all of Tahoe to hear, "Get your asses upstairs!"

We flew up to our room, knowing the wrath of God was about to come down on us.

A moment later, we could hear heavy Frankenstein footsteps climbing up the stairs, then along the hall towards us.

Tony's dad walked in and slammed the door, shaking the whole house.

He stood in front of both of us and asked in a whisper, "Well, did you get any?"

Tony started making up a story about us having sex with the girls, but his dad stopped him and said, "Spare me the details. You guys smell like puke!"

I always did like Tony's dad.

DAD'S HAIR

Why wouldn't a top-level executive working at a national aerospace company not want to look years younger, and in just one night?

Growing up in my family, you always had to expect the unexpected, like your mother performing table levitation in order to contact the spirits from the great beyond.

She was quite the celebrity during the 1970s, performing on TV shows, being featured in the weekly tabloids, and conducting seances at swanky Beverly Hills private parties.

My dad had a great sense of humor with impeccable timing, and he would always deliver the perfect word at just the right moment, making everyone laugh.

In our house, after dinner on Sundays was movie night.

It was held in our parents' bedroom, with our 20" Magnavox TV set balanced on a rickety brass mobile stand.

I became the remote control, getting up and down changing channels and adjusting the sound levels.

My mom, dad and three chihuahuas had the bed, while us kids were sprawled on the floor with our pillows, eating ice cream and watching the movie of the week.

My mom would massage my dad's head or rub his back and, as expected, he would fall asleep within the first 15 minutes of the movie.

On this one night, a TV commercial came on touting a hair dye exclusively for men, and how easy it was to use.

The ad guaranteed it would make any man look ten years younger.

My dad's hair was pretty much all gray, and my mom thought it would be a brilliant idea for him to at least try the hair dye, even though she knew his vanity would never allow it.

So, she found a clever way around that minor obstacle by sending my sister down to the corner drugstore to pick up the black hair dye kit that was advertised in the commercial.

When my sister returned, my mom mixed up the potion and gently, but thoroughly, rubbed it into my dad's hair as he slept, and while us kids watched in fear.

The next morning, we were all anxiously sitting around the kitchen table, waiting for the shit to hit the fan.

Within a few minutes, our dad walked in and sat down for his breakfast, looking 15 years younger, except for the black dyed blotches prominently displayed around his ears and forehead.

A moment of silence went by as the tension grew.

"I've decided to take the day off. Who wants to go to the beach?" he asked.

Then, everyone burst into laughter.

I'm pretty sure he always knew something like that would happen someday, being married to my mom.

THE TARGA

Every neighborhood has a kid who is a daredevil, madman, gambler, thrill-seeker, adrenaline junkie, psycho, risk-taker, crazy man, exhibitionist, knucklehead, or, who us kids knew as Mikey.

It was his insecurities that caused him to be the consummate show-off and need to impress everyone all the time.

His parents seemed to have a lot of money, or let's just say they had enough to buy a new car after every time Mikey wrecked one.

The first car on the list was his dad's eight-year-old, mint condition 1965 Porsche 912 Targa.

Mikey, being only 14 years old, and with no license or permission from his dad, asked Benny and me if we wanted to go along for a ride to show off his driving skills.

Benny and I were not the smartest of kids, so we eagerly climbed into the car and took off for the demonstration.

We arrived at the local high school and immediately did some donuts on the main campus lawn in front of the administration offices.

That didn't get much attention, so we headed for the track field.

On our second lap around the slippery dirt track, we noticed a crowd of about 20 adults running towards us and yelling, like a torch-wielding mob chasing Frankenstein.

This forced us to make a quick escape out a side gate through the teachers' parking lot and onto the street.

Having had enough excitement for one day, and not wanting to push our luck, we decided to just head back home.

Only a block away from Mikey's house, and traveling around 40 miles an hour, he was still determined to show us just how superior this Targa handled.

Going way too fast, he suddenly took a sharp left down a side street, and the car started to slide.

Mikey, with no real driving experience, over-corrected, fishtailed back and forth, and finally totally lost control.

Benny and I started screaming, thinking for sure we were going to die.

With a deafening sound, the car slammed sideways into a curb, slicing off all four tires, flying over a sidewalk and lawn, finally coming to rest in a garden of rose bushes.

At that speed, it was sheer luck the car didn't flip over.

There we were, Mikey at the wheel, Benny sitting shotgun, and me, crammed into the fold-down rear seat.

We felt motionless, like floating silently in space, as a dark cloud of dirt settled outside the car.

Reality hit us hard, like a bad medical report.

What in God's name just happened?

Here we sat, only a few doors down from Mikey's house, on the direct path that his dad would soon be driving on his way home from work, which would be any minute.

In a trembling voice, Mikey asked, "What do we do now?"

Remembering the best answer for difficult times like this, and one which had always worked for me in many past situations, I yelled, "RUN!"

We climbed out of the ruined car and did just that.

Mikey said that he couldn't go home or his dad would kill him, so I told him to follow me.

He was bawling his eyes out when we told my mom what had happened.

My mom, who the kids in the neighborhood called "Saint Pauline," consoled Mikey and told him not to worry.

She went to the living room cabinet bar, pulled out my a bottle of my dad's 12-year-old Chivas Regal, poured a tall glass, then placed it on the living room coffee table, and instructed us kids to go hide in my bedroom and lock the door.

20 minutes later, there was loud pounding on the front door, shaking the whole house as if it was about to come down.

All we could hear was Mikey's dad yelling, "Where the hell is he?"

My mom invited him into the living room, where she sat him down and gave him the tall drink of forgiveness.

We heard yelling back and forth from both of them for about an hour.

Mikey, still in one piece, finally left with his dad.

My mom was truly a miracle worker and confessed that she, herself, got in more trouble as a child than she cared to remember.

Then, she gave me these words to live by, "Shit happens."

CARPINTERIA TO HOPE RANCH

"Hello?"

"Hey, can I spend the night? I'll even buy dinner and drinks."

The voice sounded vaguely familiar.

It was deep and raspy, with a sort of chuckle behind it.

"Who is this?"

"Dude, it's me, Danny!"

Danny was a jumbo kind of guy who loved to laugh and party.

His carnival-like personality lit up a room when he walked in and, in my opinion, he was the original 'Dude.'

Back in our high school cafeteria, he once slipped four slices of ham under his plate to avoid paying for them, so my trust in him was somewhat lacking.

Not having seen or heard from this guy in years made me suspicious of how he even got my phone number, but I continued to listen to his plea.

He was calling from a restaurant in Carpinteria, a small beach community located about 15 miles south of where I lived in Santa Barbara.

At the time, my life couldn't have been better.

I had just landed a dream job and moved into a charming guest house on three wooded acres in an exclusive enclave of multi-million-dollar homes just north of downtown Santa Barbara.

I thought about his request for a moment, and agreed to meet him only because he was buying.

Our conversation was pretty much one-sided, as all he could do was talk about his life with an overabundance of superlatives and fiction.

I was quickly reminded of why I hadn't kept in touch with him.

After two hours of eating, drinking, and reminiscing about the glory days, reality set in.

How do we drive back to my place without being busted or getting into an accident?

We calculated our options.

Option one: We could take the freeway, which was the shortest but riskiest route because we might be spotted by the highway patrol, or, even worse, cause an accident.

Option two: Navigate the longer, much less traveled back roads; a safer choice but one which would take at least a half hour longer.

We never thought of the obvious option three, just call a cab.

So, I drove the long winding way home, all the while hoping that my Chevy station wagon was inconspicuous enough to avoid earning a second look as we drove through the sleepy neighborhoods.

We did see several private security vehicles disguised as police cars patrolling Montecito, which made for a very nervous ride.

What a relief it was to arrive home, safe and sound.

I told Danny he could sleep on the couch in the living room.

Upon getting ready for bed, while unraveling his backpack, four very large bricks of marijuana dropped to the floor.

"Oh my God. What the hell! Why didn't you tell me you had this shit on you?"

His moronic answer was, "Uh, I do this all the time and didn't think you would mind."

What a jerk!

We could have been busted, and sentenced to jail for years, and I wouldn't be surprised if he said all the dope was mine.

The next morning, he was already gone by the time I woke up and did a quick inspection to make sure he didn't steal anything.

I'm not sure how he got to his next destination, but I didn't care.

That's when I realized that my next free meal and drinks could have been in prison!

TABLE SURFING

One quiet summer's night, my parents were at a neighbor's party and our babysitter was in the kitchen doing her homework.

Like a lot of kids growing up in the 1960s, my brother and I were huge fans of hot rods and surfing movies, and this particular night we were watching *Muscle Beach Party*.

It got us all excited about surfing and riding the wild waves, and we decided we wanted to find something around the house to help us pretend we were surfing during the movie.

We had skateboards, but there was a rule, 'No skateboard riding in the house!'

So, we continued to look through every room until, finally, we found our make-believe surfboard!

My grandmother's antique glass-top coffee table.

It was one of the few items our family inherited after my grandmother died.

It was made around the turn of the century, and was cherished by my mom because it was the table on which she used to do her homework when she was growing up.

The small metal table was oval and measured about two feet across at its widest point, by about three feet long and two feet tall, supported by four thin decorative legs.

My brother and I were only eight and seven years old and, with neither of us having a degree in structural engineering, thought it would be our ideal make-believe surfboard.

Thinking of safety first, we both took off our socks so we wouldn't slip on the glass.

While watching the surf movie, we took turns climbing on the table, pretending we were surfing the big waves.

It was our first virtual experience.

My brother went first and did a better job than Frankie Avalon in the movie.

Then it was my turn.

I was extremely wobbly at first, but soon got the hang of it, with one foot near one end of the table, and the other foot at the opposite end.

My brother then thought it would be a cool idea to view my balancing act from underneath the table, like being underwater.

He crawled underneath and positioned himself.

Everything was going great until I shifted my weight to one foot and lifted the two front table legs off the ground.

Suddenly, I lost my balance, slamming the table down so hard that the glass exploded, causing me to fall through onto his head.

Blood started gushing from around his eyes and my feet.

I yelled for the babysitter.

She ran over in a panic and, seeing all the blood, immediately called my parents to come home.

Within seconds, both my mom and dad flew in through the front door.

The first thing I heard was the all-too-familiar greeting from my dad, "Goddammit!"

They did a quick assessment, and my dad grabbed my bloody brother and rushed him to the hospital.

My mom stayed home to clean up and bandage my legs and feet.

I sliced up my right foot, almost cutting off the two middle toes, leaving a deep scar.

My brother received stitches around his left eye and the emergency room doctor said it was a miracle he didn't lose both eyes.

Every time I notice my scar, or watch an old surfing movie, it reminds of the accident and the immortal words my dad asked us that night, and probably what every kid has heard one time or another, "What the hell were you guys thinking?"

Obviously, we weren't.

THE TROUBADOUR

I was crammed into the last row of our family's 1964 Buick station wagon, and heard my mom announce an idea that only she could have dreamt up, by stating, "Wouldn't it be wonderful if all you kids learned to play a musical instrument, and then start a band together?"

It was painful enough just to be in the same room with my siblings, let alone share a stage.

The idea of being musicians sounded exciting, but this undertaking would take years of practice, patience and dedication.

I wasn't up for the challenge, but went along with her plan anyways.

My two older brothers chose the guitar and bass guitar, while my sister would go through a multitude of instruments until she finally surrendered to the accordion.

She only chose that instrument because the instructor was drop-dead handsome, and since she was only 13 and he was 27, it made perfect sense.

I decided on the drums.

After taking lessons at a variety of music stores, and from neighborhood drum instructors, I borrowed $150 from my parents and bought a five-piece, simulated blue marble St. George drum set.

Only being eight years old, it would take me years to pay back my parents, even though it was their idea to begin with.

This drum set soon replaced hours of playing with my friends and watching TV, with hours spent practicing rudiments to a metronome alone in my bedroom instead.

Within a couple of months, both of my brothers and sister each abandoned their lessons, along with any interest in music.

I continued, and soon went on to play in the school bands, orchestras, and then with various party bands in the neighborhood.

By the age of 19, I had gotten much more serious and began scouring the local Hollywood entertainment newspapers and magazines in search of more professional players and situations.

I placed a want ad that read, "Ten years of playing drums, new equipment, a truck and access to rehearsal space."

With an ad like that, who wouldn't call me?

After receiving a number of inquiries, I was contacted by a guitarist and keyboardist, and we all decided to meet one afternoon to run through some songs and check out each other's abilities.

We sounded pretty good together, so we started adding other band members over the following weeks.

At our rehearsals, someone would bring in a new melody or some lyrics, and then the rest of the band would take it from there.

Within a couple of hours, we would have a completed song, unique to our individual styles of playing as a band.

All the members were excellent musicians and our personalities jelled nicely.

Our musical style could be considered a medley of pop, progressive rock, and jazz, with some classical influences mixed in, which made the band sound completely original.

After months of rehearsals, and with a complete 45-minute set of original songs, we were ready to record our demo.

It was my first experience in a professional recording studio and was pleasantly surprised just how good my playing and drum set sounded on 24-track tape.

We booked the band at a variety of small clubs in the San Fernando Valley and Hollywood, while building an audience of followers.

One trick I used to get people to our shows was to put an ad in the local music newspapers and magazines, seeking musicians to replace our current members.

We would tell them to just come to the show, check out the band, and then call us afterwards; but, of course, we weren't really looking for anyone, we just needed to fill seats.

On some nights, we had a full house of mostly musicians.

Once we felt that the band was ready and there was a buzz around town about us, we contacted as many record labels as we could to come see our show.

We were ready for our big breakout performance at the world-famous music venue, Doug Weston's Troubadour, located in West Hollywood.

Everybody and anybody starting out in music had played the Troubadour, from Bob Dylan, Led Zeppelin, and Elton John, to the Red-Hot Chili Peppers.

We had booked the show on a Sunday night and were the first to go on.

That was always the best slot of the night because we could leave our gear on stage after the sound check and know the PA system and everything else was set perfectly for our band.

Outside the Troubadour, the street was lined with limousines displaying record label vanity plates like Capital, A&M, Elektra, etc., as well as a large crowd of people waiting to get in.˙

That night, it was standing room only.

Not only did the band kick ass, but we came back for two encores.

We couldn't have asked for a better night and felt like rock stars!

After our performance, we returned to the stage to get our instruments and carried them out to the alley behind the club where our cars were double-parked.

We immediately noticed that the guitar player was conspicuously absent.

Moments later, he showed up and explained that a couple of record label reps approached him after the show, expressing an interest in signing the band to a record contract.

We did it!

All those hours and hours of practice and rehearsals had paid off.

We reached our goal of possibly becoming the next icon in the music industry.

Our lead singer was bold enough to ask him how the money and royalties were to be split among the band members.

Everyone assumed that it would be evenly split, but, sadly, we found out this was not the case.

The guitar player explained that since it was his idea to start and organize the band, it would come down to 60% in his favor and the remaining 40% for the other four members to share.

Like with many bands, the biggest mistake was never understanding the financials or talking about how the money, if any, would be split between all members.

We just wanted to be rock stars, and assumed all that other boring business stuff would take care of itself.

After a year of working hard to get to this point, this is what it came down to.

Regrettably, both the singer and bass player quit right then and there in the alley.

After a week of not hearing from anyone, I was informed that there was no longer a band.

Over the next year, the guitar player tried several times to start a new group using the same songs, but it never again got off the ground.

This whole experience should be the first lesson every music student needs to be taught.

Talk about the 'What if?' before you join.

And get it in writing!

THE SWEATSHIRT

I was between classes at my locker exchanging books when a girl approached me and said, "My very shy friend over there wants to meet you."

She pointed to the wall of lockers across the hallway where another girl was holding an armful of books.

After one look, I forgot how shy I was and walked over to her to introduce myself.

"Hi, I'm…"

She stopped me and said, "I know, it's Bob."

She went on and explained that she saw me a week earlier in the school's lunchtime gymnastics presentation.

It seemed strange that she already knew a lot about me, and yet, still wanted to meet me.

We talked for a couple of minutes until the class bell rang.

I was so overwhelmed that I couldn't even remember her name and was in a trance for the rest of the day.

Did I just fall in love?

At that age, I had no idea what these feelings were, and found myself drowning in uncharted waters.

Sure, I dreamt of girls 24/7, but this was way different.

I fumbled my way through a short conversation, but still managed to get her phone number.

The more I got to know her, the more I discovered there was nothing about her I wasn't crazy about.

Throughout the following year of dating, we were inseparable.

She was my Dorothy from the movie, *Summer of '42*, and had changed my world.

After graduating high school, I went to work in a local factory and she decided to travel around South America for what she called a "learning vacation."

It was the longest three weeks of my life, missing her every minute of every day that she was away.

We wrote to each other daily for about a week, and then fewer and fewer letters came until the last one.

I blamed the missing letters on the postal service.

Near the end of her trip, she called to tell me her arrival date and time, and she asked if I could pick her up at the airport.

Arriving at the airport, I learned that her flight was delayed causing me to wait for over three hours while holding two dozen white and yellow daisies, her favorites.

Her plane finally landed around 1:00 am, and I met her at the arrival gate, where she walked straight into my arms.

A small kiss and barely a hug were disappointing to say the least, especially after all this time apart.

Maybe she was just tired from her flight and all the delays.

In the car on the way home, she was very direct and wasted no time telling me she didn't feel the same about our relationship anymore, and things were going to be changing.

I can still remember the exact location where she said this to me.

We were northbound on the 405 freeway, in the number one lane, just under the Sunset Blvd. overpass.

Like in the movie, *Casablanca*, I felt like Humphrey Bogart at the train station getting his guts kicked out.

Less than a week later, she made it official and reminded me not to call or try to see her again.

I felt incredibly rejected and lost.

Maybe, somehow, I caused the breakup and questioned myself about everything.

Unfortunately, for many years I compared all other women to her, and probably missed several great opportunities for other relationships.

I just couldn't mentally or emotionally move on.

16 years later, while having a cup of coffee outside a bakery, I saw her walk into a Hallmark store across the street.

Was that really her?

She hadn't changed, except for becoming even more beautiful and sophisticated.

What was I to do, or say, if anything at all?

There she was, and here I sat.

With years of fantasizing of possibly meeting her again, I was frozen and without a plan.

Should I be mad that she had stolen 16 years of my life?

I took a deep breath, entered the store, and saw her going through the birthday card section.

She was probably picking out a card for someone she was in love with now.

I cautiously walked over to her and stammered out, "Hello."

She was stunned.

Did I scare her?

Certainly not the reaction I was expecting.

She was in a hurry but wanted to meet again and talk, so she handed me her business card and walked out the door.

A couple of days later I called, and we arranged to have lunch.

As I walked up to her workplace, I noticed three floors of about a dozen people scattered in the tall windows peering down at me.

I guess the word got out about our meeting today, or maybe she needed witnesses just in case I became violent or revengeful?

She came out, we said our hellos, and then walked to a nearby restaurant to have lunch.

During lunch, our conversation was more of a confession on her part.

She explained that she did love me once, and that she'll always remember the great times we spent together, but it had just been time for her to move on with her life.

She also felt bad that she wasn't able to handle the whole breakup a little better.

We updated each other on what we were currently doing in life, and finished our lunch.

On our walk back to her office, we passed my car, and I asked her to stop for a moment.

I started to open the trunk, and she became a little frightened and backed away.

Did she think I had a gun or knife in the car, and this was payback time?

I leaned in and pulled out an old, battered cardboard box, slowly opened it, then grabbed a crumpled plastic bag that was inside.

Out of the bag came a crimson red sweatshirt that read Ohio State University.

She was born in Ohio, and she always talked about going back there one day.

She asked, "OMG, did you buy this especially for our lunch today?"

"No. I bought it on the way to the airport that day you arrived home, but never had the chance to give it to you. I've carried it around in every car I've owned, just in case one day I might see you again."

I handed her the sweatshirt.

She smiled and gave me a final hug, turned, and walked away for the last time.

As I watched her, an unfamiliar emotion came over me.

I finally stopped feeling sorry for myself, and now knew I had a full life in front of me after all.

PHOTOS IN CHURCH

I took it upon myself to host a bachelor party for a good friend because it was the least someone could do for this reluctant groom-to-be.

We knew his marriage wouldn't last, but agreed he deserved at least a proper sendoff for his efforts.

By 8:00 p.m., my little one-bedroom apartment became an arena with wall-to-wall guys.

Most of them didn't even care who the bachelor was, but free beer and a stripper were all they needed to show up.

I hired an exotic dancer from a local entertainment service, and at around 9:00 p.m. the doorbell rang.

The room froze with anticipation as I answered the door.

There stood a seven-foot-tall bodyguard escorting a gorgeous petite blonde wearing a revealing red and white nurse's outfit.

This fantasy caregiver would heal anyone just by walking into the room.

I introduced her to the bachelor, and she graciously took it from there.

A true professional.

She led my friend to the center of the room, slowly unbuttoned his shirt, and threw it to the crowd.

Then she removed his shoes, sensually unbuckled his pants, slid them down his legs, and tossed them aside.

At this point, the bachelor and I both started to worry she might go too far.

A few of the guys gathered up all his clothes, soaked them in the kitchen sink, and stuck them in the freezer.

We figured this would help him cool off after the stripper's performance.

She sat him down on one of my small kitchen chairs and handcuffed his wrists together behind his back.

Then she proceeded to give him a very erotic lap dance while removing her little nurse's uniform down to her sexy red lingerie, fishnet stockings, and stiletto heels.

As she danced, the guys were cheering her on like it was the fourth down, two yards to go.

To show off her tan shapely legs, she lifted up her left foot and placed it onto my antique coffee table.

As she set it down, her red spike heel broke the glass top, shattering it to pieces.

The whole room gawked at me for my reaction.

Thrusting my beer bottle high into the air, I yelled, "Keep going!"

Another roar came from the gallery.

When her show was over, everyone chipped in and tipped her handsomely for her unique talent.

The bachelor party was a big success and, luckily, nobody got hurt.

Throughout the entire night, I took dozens of photos so the bachelor would have an enduring remembrance of his last night of freedom.

Excited to see the photos myself, I took the film to a one-hour photo store the next morning.

I returned to pick up the photos on my way to the church so I could give them to the groom at the reception.

As I sat in the packed house of worship, waiting for the wedding to begin, a friend next to me asked, "So, how was the party last night?"

"Take a look for yourself," and I handed him the photos.

His eyes lit up as he rifled through them and before I could stop him, he passed them to the guy sitting next to him.

Within minutes, the photos were circulating throughout the entire chapel, like an empty collection plate.

The priest even stopped the ceremony a couple of times just to see what the commotion was all about.

That was the last time I saw the evidence, or my former friend, the groom.

THE NAPKIN PUPPET

It started out as just another uneventful black-tie affair with the usual cocktail hour, five-course dinner, and annual presentations.

This night, a group of prominent psychiatrists were having their annual holiday party and awards ceremony at a very luxurious hotel in Santa Barbara, California.

I was hired to play drums in a five-piece combo that included some exceptional musicians and featured a well-known jazz pianist.

After all the guests had cocktails and dinner, the host graciously offered the band dinner while the doctors gave out awards and lectured about medical breakthroughs in their fields of expertise.

The band's table was on stage left, behind large curtains and hidden from the view of the audience.

The last presenter came up and gave a short talk about a particular patient of his who had been suffering from depression and anxiety his whole life.

He explained how the patient had achieved an incredible recovery by learning to play the piano and, with such great progress, now had the confidence to leave his house for the first time in years.

The recovering patient was then invited onto the stage where a grand piano was set up especially for him.

He appeared to be nervous as he rose from his seat, and made his way to the piano bench, all the while glancing back at our band.

114

Listening to our keyboardist during the first two hours must have been extremely intimidating, as well as this being his first performance in front of a live audience.

The fragile patient looked at the piano's keyboard for a moment, took a deep breath, and then began to play.

I had finished my dinner before the rest of the band and, feeling bored, created a simple napkin puppet to amuse myself.

My puppet danced to the patient's song, and was held just high enough for only my bandmates to see.

The band tried to stifle their giggles, but the giggling soon turned into laughter.

The more they tried to stop, the harder it was for them to keep quiet.

Unfortunately, the patient could see all of us laughing, and obviously thought it was because of his playing.

He started missing notes, and then, suddenly, stopped playing altogether and ran out of the ballroom in a panic.

Then, the room went silent as everyone looked at each other in disbelief of what had just occurred.

If you happen to be that patient reading this story, I just want to say that I am really sorry.

Obviously, I'm the one who should have received some psychiatric help!

THE CHRISTMAS DOLL

I landed a dream job as the art director for a small Santa Barbara-based startup company that created very popular children's interactive computer games.

It employed a collection of very talented coworkers and practical jokers.

Weeks before Christmas, our boss suggested a Secret Santa gift exchange for the upcoming holiday party.

Everyone thought that would be a great idea, so we all drew names from a hat to learn who we had to buy a present for.

The rules were that the gift must be appropriate for that individual, but it also had to be funny in some way.

The party was to be held at one of the many restaurants located on the picturesque Santa Barbara pier.

The weather was perfect for a sunny California Christmas party.

With the afternoon off to partake in a free meal and drinks, everyone was definitely in the holiday spirit.

My giftee was a computer programmer who constantly complained about all the hard work he had to do, while always carrying around a half-empty bottle of water.

I guess he wanted to give the impression that he was exhausted and dehydrated from all the typing on his keyboard.

All the programmers I've known live in a strange world all their own.

But what would we do without them?

My carefully chosen gift to him was a packet of cheap vitamins from 7-Eleven and a six-pack of bottled water.

He didn't think it was funny, but that didn't matter, the entire company did.

When it came to the gift I was given, there were instructions to first read the attached poem out loud before the unwrapping.

The short poem with its rhyming verses was about a lonely, middle-aged, single guy, living with two cats, which perfectly describe me.

It was now time to open the present.

I peeled back the gift paper and soon discovered that it was a plastic blow-up sex doll, and immediately stopped.

There was a roar from the audience for me to continue.

As the wrapper hit the floor, I held up the clear plastic box with the folded doll inside.

The entire, and I mean the entire, crowded restaurant of patrons and staff, exploded in laughter.

If that wasn't bad enough, the doll's mouth was completely open and ready for action.

Totally embarrassed, I turned as red as the doll's lips.

Apparently, our female 3D artist had bought the gift for me, which was even more hilarious because everyone in the company thought we were dating.

I could have just thrown the doll away, but instead saved it for next year's Christmas party.

The doll was re-gifted several times thereafter, and rumor has it that someone eventually filled it with helium and launched it skyward over the ocean.

Hopefully, it landed on a deserted island where it could be truly appreciated and cared for in a more loving way.

THE LEDGE

If there is anything I've learned, it's the difference between how men and women get over relationship breakups.

Rumor has it that women can get over a relationship in one night with a large bowl of ice cream and a good chick flick.

Whereas a guy needs to get drunk with his buddies and pour his guts out as if he's dying of an incurable disease.

Benny frantically called and confessed, "My girlfriend just told me it's over, so I'm going to commit suicide. Do you want to watch? I'm buying."

Free beer and the possibility of watching your best friend die, I'm all in.

"Yes! Can I bring a friend?"

I called my buddy, Tony, and he quickly came over and we all piled into Benny's brand-new car and went straight to the liquor store.

We knew the entire blame fell on Benny's shoulders because his girlfriend was a real sweetheart who finally wised up and just stopped putting up with his bullshit.

He bought us a 12-pack, and we headed to Malibu, drinking all the way there.

Unfortunately, part of the deal was that we also had to listen to Benny's broken heart story.

Tony and I did our best to give the illusion that we cared, like supplying comments such as, "You're kidding? You can do better. Wow, that is so unfair! What a bitch!"

We finally arrived at the coast and noticed a new construction site for a future campus high on a hill just above Malibu Canyon Road.

There was an opening in a steel link fence, surrounding what appeared to be a cement foundation for a large building.

We drove through it, quickly jumped out, and ran behind a yellow forklift to relieve our bladders.

We then sat on a pile of wooden pallets, and enjoyed the crystal-clear ocean view and the distant lights of Los Angeles.

Benny began to explain in agonizing detail why the best way to get back at the old girlfriend was to commit suicide.

Seeing how pathetic he was acting, I now started to agree with him.

"Sure! Go for it. In fact, do it in front of her. That will show her!"

Suddenly, out of nowhere, four bright headlights blinded us.

Then, two flashing red and blue lights lit up on the top of the car.

"Oh shit, we're busted!"

Through a large cloud of dirt came a looming shadow holding a flashlight and God-knows-what else.

Yep, it was the sheriff.

He saw all the beer cans, asked what we were doing, and then gave Benny the sobriety test, twice.

He barely passed both times.

When Benny started telling the sheriff his sob story, the officer abruptly told him to shut up.

Apparently, he heard enough too.

The officer then informed us that he was scheduled to get off work in fifteen minutes, and that if he took us down to the station he could book us for trespassing, but that would take at least an hour.

He generously offered us an unbelievable option.

He said, "Clean up your beer cans and drive straight back to the Valley, and I never want to see you guys again."

We all thankfully agreed.

Of course, that didn't happen.

After the sheriff left, we cleaned up our mess and left the construction site, but instead of driving home, we decided to get something to eat at the 24-hour Jack in the Box across from the Malibu Pier.

We went through the drive-thru and ordered.

Within minutes, we were handed our food.

Tony was checking the contents of his bag when he found that they gave him a strawberry malt instead of a chocolate one.

For some strange reason, he came unglued and began yelling at the cashier in the drive-thru window, and then threw the malt back inside where it splattered everywhere.

I could see the manager frantically calling the police.

Benny throttled the car out of the driveway sideways, as if we were filming a scene from *Smokey and the Bandit*.

Turning south on Pacific Coast Highway, the car rocketed to over 100 miles an hour through traffic lights while passing cars in the adjacent lane.

At times, the car seemed to take flight and lift off the ground.

As Tony and I were saying our prayers, Benny turned to me and yelled, "If you guys were my friends, you'd die with me tonight!"

He was a good friend, but not enough to give up my life for him or his old girlfriend.

I finally talked him down off the ledge by telling him I could fix him up with my girlfriend's sister who was last year's Playmate of the Year.

She didn't have a sister, but being truthful at that moment was the least of my concerns.

He immediately slowed down the car, and we eventually made it home in one piece.

I think the next time a friend gets dumped, I'll recommend professional help, or at least take away their car keys.

THE LAVATORY

The original plan was that after my band's rehearsal, I would drive to a fashionable bistro to meet some friends for a quiet night of dinner and drinks.

The restaurant was about 30 minutes away from the rehearsal studio, which was just enough time to guzzle down a couple of beers on the way over.

This way, I could walk in with a buzz and not have to spend so much money on alcohol.

As I was driving up to the corner where the club was located, there were two police officers in their car stopped at the traffic light across the intersection.

Being extremely paranoid and nervous after already drinking the beers, I'll just play it cool, not look their way, drive the correct speed limit, and navigate straight through like a good driver.

As I drove through the intersection and past them, it suddenly dawned on me the reason they were stopped.

It was because the traffic light was red for them, which also meant it was red for me.

Out of the corner of my eye, I could see them looking at me, wondering why in hell would someone deliberately run a red light in front of police?

It didn't take them long to figure out the answer.

They immediately turned on their lights and siren while making a U-turn after me.

I had about an 80-yard lead on them, so I stomped on the gas, turned off my lights, flew into the restaurant's parking lot, raced around to the back of the building, and, luckily, parked in the only spot open.

Crawling on my hands and knees through a long hedge of adjacent bushes, I could see the police car race past me.

At the front of the restaurant, I stood up brushing off all the dirt and leaves, and then calmly walked straight to the men's bathroom.

I entered, and again, luckily, found the only vacant stall, and took a seat.

A few minutes later, the bathroom door flew open, slamming against the wall with a deafening bang.

Oh no, I'm trapped with nowhere to go.

I immediately started grunting loudly, as if I was passing a huge cactus.

Two men were at the door mumbling back and forth, so I continued my straining noises until the door finally closed.

After about 20 minutes, and smelling like Pine-Sol, I emerged from the bathroom into the crowded restaurant to meet my friends.

My friend said, "Dude, you missed all the action. Two cops came running through the place looking for someone, and they were really pissed off."

"Yeah, too bad I missed that."

GOOD MORNING BURRITO

I was on autopilot; working in a factory nine hours a day, playing drums three or four nights a week and, with whatever time left, taking college courses.

My musical gigs or rehearsals usually ended around midnight, after which I had to pack up my drums, drive home, and then carry them up a full flight of stairs into my small apartment.

My day job started at 6 a.m., which left little time for a good night's sleep or a well-balanced diet.

After the morning alarm went off, I quickly dressed, flew out the door, and usually picked up some food on the way to work.

My favorite breakfast was the classic Tommy's chili cheeseburger with onions and Jalapeno peppers.

If that didn't jump start your day, nothing would.

This 24-hour fast-food restaurant was conveniently located on my way to work, leaving me just enough time to inhale the burger before arriving at the company parking lot.

This morning, I was running late and regrettably didn't have time to stop.

I ran to my workstation just as the shop bell rang.

Confined to my work area for the next three hours, and starving like a stray dog, I was desperate.

About 30 yards away were the vending machines which offered pre-made snacks, sandwiches and salads, as well as coffee, soft drinks and just about anything else you could think of.

The coffee, which only cost a quarter, had the added benefit of clearing your digestive tract like a colonoscopy.

My hunger pains convinced me that the vending machines were my only hope of getting through the morning.

If I could do my work quickly, it would give me a little extra time to go check out anything worth eating.

I did just that, and ran to the machines.

After reviewing all my options, I hastily decided on the beef and cheese burrito, only because on the wrapper were three pretty, smiling señoritas who looked like they all took pride in cooking the food themselves.

I bought the burrito and threw it into the microwave, then ran back to my workstation to work ahead again, making enough time for grabbing my hot breakfast from the oven.

During this ballet, my supervisor was watching me intensely, making sure my job was being done without mistakes.

I was beyond hungry at this point, and felt relieved to have something to eat.

Peeling back the paper-wrapped burrito released a steamy vapor of stench which filled my work area.

The smell was like opening a warm coffin in El Paso.

I asked my Hispanic co-worker if this was how these burritos should smell.

He made a repugnant face and said he would never eat Mexican food from a vending machine, and that I was taking my life into my own hands.

He was no help.

I just held my breath and took a large bite.

It tasted like that El Paso corpse.

The more I ate, the worse it got, but being so hungry, I was determined to finish the whole thing.

The goo was hard to swallow, almost choking me.

Halfway through the burrito, I tore back the remaining wrapper only to find the second half was saturated with green mold and dead maggots.

I barfed out what I had in my mouth and started gagging.

My foreman came running over and told me to hurry to the bathroom to finish my purge.

All I could think about were those three pretty señoritas who, apparently, are now laughing instead of just smiling.

PAYBACK

Every Friday, after our high school track competitions, some of the team members would meet up at my parents' garage for our exclusive biology experiment.

Running all day in the heat and sweating off five pounds, we would drink one beer to see how much of a buzz we would get.

Yes, just one.

It wasn't very scientific, but we got the results we wanted.

My parents' house had a three-car garage, and was located at the end of a cul-de-sac with an unobstructed view of all the comings and goings in the neighborhood, which made for the perfect hangout.

My mom liked these gatherings because she knew where we were, and was always willing to feed everyone.

Early in the week, each kid would buy their own imported beer, put their name on it, and store it in an old refrigerator in our garage.

There was this one kid, Tim, who was a real prankster in the group.

To Tim, no joke was too cruel or off limits.

As an example, just to get a laugh, he once lit my hair on fire in class for no reason.

We all decided we had enough of his antics and came up with an idea for a prank to play on him.

During the week, we carefully opened Tim's beer, poured out the contents, and then replaced it with a special brew.

We filled the bottle with spit, dirt, lawn clippings and topped it off with some fresh dog poop.

I meticulously put the cap back on so you couldn't tell it had been tampered with, and placed it back in the refrigerator along side the other bottles.

After Friday's track meet, we all met back at my garage.

As everyone popped their lids off, I quickly interrupted and said, "Wait! Let's not just drink our beers, let's guzzle them."

Everyone agreed, and then I yelled, "Go!"

All eyes were on Tim as he gulped down his modified brew.

With his head bent back, his Adam's apple quickly went to work.

In less than two seconds, he lunged forward as brown chunky liquid exploded out of his mouth and nose.

He collapsed to the ground, face first, into some rose bushes.

I thought we were going to lose him after a period of intense convulsions, and then lying motionless for a minute or two.

Finally getting his breath back, he mumbled some profanity and staggered home, although leaning to one side.

Lesson learned, never let your beer out of your sight.

INSULT TO INJURY

I never saw Jerry with an actual girlfriend, and never questioned it, except once, when a girl ran up and started screaming at him in front of the entire high school.

This was unexpected and frightening, to say the least.

Jerry was our high school's basketball star.

He was handsome, a cross between George Clooney and Pierce Brosnan, with Johnny Carson's wit and charm.

One afternoon, we were walking to our next class along a very congested outdoor corridor when, out of nowhere, and without warning, a girl came at us like a sniper's bullet.

She had a pair of long black pigtails, a mouth filled with railroad tracks, and a body that you couldn't tell whether it was coming or going.

I can only assume she must have had other great attributes.

She pounced within inches of Jerry's face, and began yelling at him at the top of her lungs.

"How come you never call me? You never even say hi! Can you hear me inside that stupid head of yours? You're just using me! Hello!"

As she ranted, a crowd of our classmates gathered around and started following us as we kept walking, trying to do our best to ignore her.

She was walking backwards in front of us this entire time, yelling and flapping her arms around in the air like an injured bird falling from a tree.

At one point, she bumped it up a notch and grabbed Jerry's shirt, ripping off three of the buttons.

Jerry only smiled, hoping this banshee would simply evaporate on her own.

After a long, one-sided screaming fest, she let out her last two words, "F-YOU!"

The poor thing then quickly turned around, directly into an eight-inch-wide metal pole that was supporting the walkway's roof.

The clang of her skull hitting this hollow pillar was very loud, like a hammer striking a bell ending a boxing match.

She ricocheted down onto the concrete path.

The growing audience following us erupted in laughter, and then applauded her performance.

This embarrassed, exhausted girl then grabbed her bruised cranium and ran off crying.

After class, I asked Jerry if he had an explanation for this girl's actions.

He confessed, "We agreed that every day at lunch for the past three months we would sneak off to her parents' house just to 'make-out.' Other than that, I didn't want to have anything else to do with her. So, now I'm really confused."

Mystery solved.

THE RED-EYE

With an angry flight crew, a female circus performer, two rock 'n' roll musicians, three salesmen, and a plane full of sleeping passengers on a midnight flight to a city in the South, what could possibly go wrong?

Because of my irrational fear of flying, my guitarist and I arrived at the airport early to have a couple of beers before our scheduled red-eye.

He was a colorful fashion nugget who resembled a cross between Prince and Madonna, with a little of Jimi Hendrix thrown in.

We were on our way to record our band's first album.

Fortunately, my carry-on luggage, which had an extra six-pack of beer for the trip, was not thoroughly inspected.

When we got on the plane, we soon discovered that everyone had already boarded and was settling in for the night.

We didn't know anything about pre-booking our seats, and ended up at the very back of the plane, where two rows of three seats faced each another.

To my left was my guitarist and to my right was a cute, shoeless 19-year-old gal wearing an elaborate gypsy outfit with her hair tied up in multicolored ribbons.

I asked her about her outfit and she said she had just come from working in a traveling circus and was on her way home for the holidays.

Sitting across from us were three traveling salesmen.

One sold canned vegetables, and another strictly fresh fruit.

Sitting in-between them was an insurance agent, wearing the loudest plaid jacket money could buy.

None of the three salesmen had much fashion sense, but they certainly knew how to party.

When I told them we were up-and-coming rock stars on our way to becoming famous, they just laughed.

Around three in the morning, we were still drinking and making so much noise that the flight attendant told us to be quiet or she would inform the pilot, who could then have us arrested when we touched down at our destination.

Too drunk to realize the seriousness of the situation, we continued to drink and make fools of ourselves.

20 minutes later, the pilot, with his headset still on, marched up the aisle through the dark sleeping plane toward us.

He leaned into our party and growled, "If you guys don't shut up, I'll have you thrown in jail when we land!"

We all apologized and said we were extremely sorry and promised to quiet down.

The angry and frustrated pilot turned and started back to the cockpit.

Stupidly, I yelled, "Hey! Who's flying the plane?"

Wow, that woke everyone up!

Scores of sleepy passengers turned on their overhead lights and started looking out their windows, expecting the worst.

The pilot stopped, turned around, pointed directly at me, and then disappeared into the cockpit.

Our group immediately settled down for the rest of the flight.

However, I soon started to panic because our destination was in the deep South, and lord knows what kind of justice or treatment we might receive there.

Luckily, when we arrived, there were no air marshals or police.

Just a couple of local news reporters, and a long black limousine with half a dozen southern babes dressed like strippers waving from the sunroof.

The three salesmen couldn't believe their eyes, and gave us the thumbs up.

My career choice was once again affirmed.

A Rock Star in the making!

THE SHOWERS

My best friend and I invented the most immature and embarrassing prank that everyone needs to try at least once in their lifetime.

When large house parties got dull and boring, we would grab some beers and hide in a bathroom shower.

I told you it was immature.

With drinks in hand, we would step into the shower, pull the curtain or door closed, and then stand or sit quietly while waiting for an unsuspecting victim to walk in.

Once they were in the room, we would yell, "Boo!" and scare the hell out of them.

It's the last thing anyone would expect to happen in the privacy of a bathroom.

Yes, this was childish, stupid, and silly, but what wasn't when you were a kid, so why not as an adult?

We tried never to let it go too far because that would be perverted, and maybe even against the law, although, remember, we were in the bathroom first.

The very first time we tried this prank was back in high school, at our friend's large birthday party.

We snuck into the shower, pulled the curtain, and waited.

Fortunately, or unfortunately, we didn't have to wait too long, but we were totally unprepared for what happened next.

Our first victim was a very cute gal who flew into the bathroom, shut the door, and sat down before we even had a chance to utter a word.

Although we couldn't see or hear anything, we had to stuff the hanging towels in our mouths to keep from laughing.

Now, that felt too weird, so we really needed to be more alert next time.

At another party, my friend grabbed me and another guy, and pulled us both into a small utility bathroom shower.

Large towels were hung over the glass, which served to hide us fairly well.

Our first guest just happened to be my girlfriend at the time.

She walked in, shut the door, checked her makeup, adjusted her hair, and quickly left.

Luckily, she didn't see us or I would have never heard the end of it.

We were laughing so much it was hard to breathe, but we managed to stifle our giggles enough not to be found out by our next victim.

Another gal walked in and shut the door.

We were caught a bit off guard, but I quickly whispered, "Boo!"

She looked straight at us, screamed, and flew out of there like she just saw three rapists.

We were like The Three Stooges trying to get out of a British phone booth, practically breaking the glass door during our escape.

We went into the living room and quickly sat down, pretending as if we had been there the whole night.

Suddenly, the girl we had scared burst into the room flanked by her oversized football player boyfriend who was grunting like a bull.

She pointed at us and shouted, "Those are the guys!"

I started to laugh because it wasn't like we saw her naked or anything, but apparently, she felt extremely violated.

The Hulk demanded that we apologize and leave the party, or he was going to beat the hell out of us.

I was a little taken aback by his macho attitude and quickly told him to kiss my ass.

As expected, that didn't go over well.

He came at me with his fist raised and yelled, "I'm going to rip your head off!"

"Sure, I'll fight you, but let's go outside so we don't mess up the house."

I led him to the front door and politely allowed him to walk out first.

Once he was outside, I immediately shut the door and locked it.

He banged on the door and almost took it off the hinges.

Everyone in the house erupted in laughter.

I quickly ran around to make sure all the other doors in the house were also locked.

The Hulk was too embarrassed now and started walking away down the street, so his girlfriend ran after him like he was an injured puppy.

At another party, a singer in a band that I was a member of hosted a large open house with about 60 guests.

My date for the party happened to be the singer's beautiful little sister, who was a junior high school teacher.

With her silver-rimmed glasses and long blonde hair, she was the epitome of why boys develop crushes on their teachers.

The party was in full swing when I asked her if she would like to do something fun.

After suggesting the prank, she looked at me very strangely for a moment, smiled, and agreed.

I took her hand and led her to the downstairs bathroom, but she insisted that we go to the master bathroom instead because it had a larger shower.

Once there, we turned off the lights and climbed into the marble and glass enclosure.

Less than two seconds later, we were making out like a couple of high school kids behind the bleachers on a Friday night.

After ten minutes of steaming up the shower glass, we heard a crowd of people coming up the stairs.

They were all heading in our direction.

Oh no, was everyone getting a tour of the new house?

We couldn't escape because there was no place to go without being busted.

We were trapped.

I hoped they would skip the master bath and check out a different room first.

The lights flipped on, and we heard a loud, "Surprise!"

I was completely red-faced and totally embarrassed.

My date started laughing and told me to turn around.

There was a large photo of my face inside a red circle with a diagonal line drawn through it.

Below, it read, "No Bobs Allowed!"

Everyone was in on the joke except me.

This threw a lot of cold water on what turned out to be my last shower hiding prank.

THE BIG WHEEL

After a high school party, my friend, Tony, suggested we spend the night up the coast near Ventura Harbor, to watch the professional drag boat races the next day.

He didn't have a car, but I had a motorcycle.

A midnight ride, especially in late September, would be freezing, but being young and foolish we were up for the adventure.

We packed my trusted green 1972 Honda CB 500 motorcycle with our sleeping bags, donned our warmest clothing, and took off into the freezing darkness.

With two people and all that gear, it made for a very unstable freeway ride, especially when Tony kept falling asleep now and then, listing the bike from side-to-side.

I had to reach back and slap his leg a couple of times to wake him up.

When we reached McGrath State Beach, we noticed our beanie caps and woolen scarves had flown off somewhere along the way.

We quietly rode through the entire campground, and finally parked in the only open spot.

Exhausted from the ride, we unrolled our ice-cold sleeping bags, crawled in, and literally passed out.

It seemed just moments later a loud noise woke me up, like someone was grinding rocks in a hollow plastic bucket.

I peeked out of my sleeping bag into the glaring sunrise to see a small boy riding a Big Wheel toy tricycle in and around our camp.

The Big Wheel was a very popular, low-riding toy that was made of yellow, red, and blue hard plastic.

The bike was almost completely hollow, and so rolling on any surface made the toy sound like thunder.

The kid probably saw my motorcycle and just wanted to show off his riding skills.

He kept circling our sleeping bags while making some growling sounds, like he was going through the gears of his own motorcycle.

I crawled deeper into my cocoon, hoping the light, and the kid, would go away.

But that didn't happen.

"What the hell!" Tony mumbled angrily.

I peered out again and saw Tony standing there in his boxer shorts.

He very politely asked the boy if he could look at his Big Wheel tricycle.

The excited boy jumped off and proudly pushed his ride towards Tony.

Tony smiled as he slowly bent down, grabbing the handlebar with one hand.

He picked up the kid's tricycle and proceeded to do an Olympian-worthy half twirl discus throw.

That Big Wheel flew 30 feet into some thick bushes and made a big splash.

The little boy, now in a state of shock, took off running.

Tony calmly crawled back into his sleeping bag like nothing happen.

I slithered deeper into my bag, with thoughts of being arrested or beaten up by the kid's father.

Fortunately, that never happened.

If that little kid, who is a grown man today, is reading this story, I hope you learned your lesson.

MOVING DAY

It didn't take me long to learn that my beautiful, brand new 1976 Chevy Scottsdale pickup truck would sometimes be more of a curse than a blessing.

At least once or twice a month, invariably, someone wanted to borrow my truck to move, or to haul something to the dump.

Since it was my pride and joy, I wouldn't think of loaning it out to anyone, and so, ultimately, I always ended up personally helping these people.

This morning, I got a desperate call from a friend, pleading his case that he had to move immediately.

He explained that his college classes were starting tomorrow, and today was the only chance he had to move into his new apartment near the campus.

To me, just the very nature of being accepted into college would imply that you would at least be smart enough to know not to wait until the last minute to move.

But what do I know?

Maybe colleges and universities had lower entrance requirements back then.

It was one of the hottest days on record in the San Fernando Valley, but I reluctantly agreed to help, and met him at his apartment.

It was a second-floor bachelor pad, with an excellent view of the pool area where, today, there just happened to be several lovely ladies in string bikinis sunbathing on lounge chairs.

It was easy to see why he had been living there, but hard to understand why he wanted to leave.

With the sweat dripping from our foreheads in the sweltering heat, we attacked the job of moving him out.

The girls were monitoring our every move up and down the stairs, probably because we were tan, shirtless, and in the best shape of our lives.

Some of them rolled over sensually now and then, just to tease us.

It certainly worked.

We first moved the smaller items, like boxes full of clothes and dishes, then came the big stuff like his grandmother's old TV and ratty sofa.

The very last item was his twin-size bed.

The box spring was easy to move quickly down the stairs and onto my truck.

However, coming down the stairs with the mattress was a bit challenging.

As it became more wobbly, somehow, the fitted sheet fell off.

Immediately, the girls started laughing hysterically.

Maybe we reminded them of Laurel and Hardy?

I discovered that wasn't it at all, and, unfortunately, saw the reason they were laughing.

OMG!

The fallen sheet had exposed the mattress, which, apparently, was the same one he grew up with as a child.

It was adorned with about 100 rust-colored pee stains in the middle section.

Being so shocked myself, I accidentally let go of the mattress at my end, and it tumbled down the stairs and straight into the pool.

The girls screamed as it hit the water, splashing them.

We ran out the gate and sped away as fast as we could, leaving the sinking mattress in the pool.

You'd think someone smart enough to get into college would know when to buy a new bed!

ROAD RAGE

After the four of us feasted on a dinner of sushi and sake, we were having an uneventful drive home on Highway 154, which connects Santa Barbara to the Santa Ynez Valley.

It's nicknamed "Blood Alley," because of the many fatal car accidents that occur on it every year.

Since we overindulged on alcohol, my girlfriend, who doesn't drink, took it upon herself to be our designated driver, which we all gladly agreed upon.

Along this desolate and winding two-lane mountainous road, suddenly, a large group of vehicles began tailgating us.

What appeared to be two motorcycles, rode up to within a few feet of our rear bumper, as their headlights lit up the inside of our car like a scene from the movie, *E.T.*

Having a bit too much to drink, I immediately flew into road rage mode.

I instructed my girlfriend to either turn on the windshield wiper sprayer or do a brake check.

She smartly ignored both of those requests, and rattled off something about my repressed anger issues and the need for professional help.

I couldn't just sit there and do nothing, so I opened the window and gave them the one-finger salute.

That didn't do anything except get the motorcycles' high beams to light up and follow even closer, almost touching our bumper.

Then, I picked up the Kleenex box from the floor, whereby my girlfriend yelled, "Don't you dare!"

Finally, about five miles down the road, we came to a long straightaway, which the convoy behind us quickly took advantage of.

With military precision, they started passing us.

I was going to yell something at them as they drove by, until I saw that they were two highway patrol motorcycles, followed by two sheriff passenger vans full of prisoners, then two more patrol cars, and finally another set of motorcycles bringing up the rear.

Thank God I was not driving!

My girlfriend was right, as usual.

I do need help.

MONKEY ON FIRE

The plan was to impress my friend, by inviting him to his first home-cooked Thanksgiving dinner, and to show off my culinary expertise.

Since he had recently moved from England to America, this would have been a great introduction to an beloved American tradition.

Watching my mom cook our family's Thanksgiving dinners many times over the years, I assumed it couldn't be that difficult.

Although, I did end up calling her about a dozen times during the process, just to refresh my memory.

My girlfriend oversaw adorning our card table with holiday decorations.

It turned out more magical than anything featured in Vanity Fair or Good Housekeeping magazines, with Grandmother's fine china, crystal, gold-plated flatware, white linen napkins, an autumn floral centerpiece, holiday-scented candles in cut glass holders, and a sterling silver gravy boat.

I spent all morning preparing and cooking, so when my friend arrived, everything was ready and on the table as he walked in.

The last thing you want is to bore your guests with watching the preparation of the meal.

After gorging ourselves on turkey, cranberry sauce, stuffing, mashed potatoes and gravy, I returned to the kitchen to layout the buffet of ice cream, fresh fruit, a variety of nuts, and pound cake.

This way, everyone could create their own work of art confection.

As we gathered around, loading up our dessert plates, we started to smell something burning, and it didn't smell like food.

I ran back into the dining room and saw my big fluffy orange cat on the table, with his body buried deep into the turkey's half-eaten carcass.

The only thing you could see was his wagging tail.

He was so focused on that large bird, he didn't notice that the fur on his sides had caught fire from the flickering candles.

I yelled his name, "Monkey!"

He took off running, racing from room to room throughout the entire two-bedroom apartment, with all of us chasing after him.

The fireball finally jumped on my bed, where I immediately threw a blanket over him.

I checked him out from head to toe, and found that practically all his fur had been singed, but otherwise, he was in good shape.

I had to explain to my friend that Feline Flambé wasn't part of the tradition.

THE VIDEO

I joined an extraordinary rock band during the early 1980s.

The songs were original, the musicians were exceptional, and every time we played live, we always got at least one standing ovation.

But, the most memorable times with this particular band weren't always on stage.

The lead singer was habitually theatrical and a consummate clown.

He always insisted on being the center of attention by incessantly playing practical jokes on everyone.

There was no prank that went too far, or too low, or was too embarrassing for the unsuspecting victim.

He was tall, handsome, and sported a mohawk haircut that would change colors more often than I changed my shirts.

One time, in an upscale Hollywood restaurant, there was a popular TV show wrap party seated at a table adjacent to ours.

The group kept staring, laughing, and pointing at our lead singer while making comments among themselves, and it was obvious that their remarks were directed at him.

Not to be intimidated, he climbed on the table, pulled down his jeans and hung a perfectly executed BA, which made the party abruptly leave.

Another memorable night, at the Roxy Theatre on the Sunset Strip, our performance was professionally videotaped.

After the show, I asked the lead singer for a copy of the tape, and he said he would drop one off at my apartment as soon as it was finished being edited.

A few days later, there was the videotape waiting for me inside my screen door.

I was shocked to discover that the first two minutes consisted of gay porn before the recording of our show started.

I then soon realized that he had added the porn as a practical joke.

I decided to return the favor by calling his phone when he wasn't home, and leaving a long-winded message on his answering machine.

It went something like this: "I'm sorry, I don't know what I did to deserve this practical joke. I have always been proud to be in your band, and couldn't wait to show our Roxy performance to everyone at my family's Thanksgiving dinner party. My family, godparents, and friends were all anxious to see the band that I so raved about. As soon as I put in the tape and pushed play, I was never so embarrassed in my life. Everyone stared at me in shock, and then quickly left the room. I tried to explain that it was probably just a practical joke, but they wouldn't listen. I just want to say 'thank you' for making my family's holiday dinner one of the worst experiences of my life."

Then, I called everyone else in the band and told them about my message, and to play along with my joke.

In the coming days, there must have been 20 recordings on my answering machine from our singer, apologizing profusely to the point that he was crying.

He asked me repeatedly to call him back, but I continued to let him suffer until our following Monday night rehearsal.

I arrived at the studio early, set up my drums, and, along with the rest of the band, waited for our singer to show up.

He finally walked in, stood in the middle of the room, and confessed, "Listen, everyone. I played a very cruel joke on Bob, and I am truly sorry. From the bottom of my heart, I am incredibly regretful and have been miserable all weekend just thinking of how I must have hurt you. I am so very, very sorry."

The whole room went silent, and nobody moved until I said, "For what?"

He replied, "That I was a total idiot and embarrassed you in front of your whole family with the gay porn on that tape."

I then responded with a smirk, "It never happened. No one saw it except me. I just made the whole thing up."

The entire band erupted in laughter, and our singer stormed out of the room dropping the "F" bomb the whole way.

Ten minutes later, he came back in, smiling, "Just wait, I'll get you back."

He never did.

Regrettably, the band broke up a short time later, as some of the players went on to play with major groups in the industry.

Even much sadder was that our lead singer died a few years later, and I never had the chance to say goodbye to him.

Although, I was able to tell this story at his wake, which filled the house with laughter, and I know he would have loved that.

JAW SURGERY

It was our first date, and everything seemed almost perfect.

At an elegant restaurant in Beverly Hills with the best-looking girl in town, having an excellent conversation until she commented, "Wow, your teeth make you look like a vampire!"

I was a little surprised and taken aback by her comment, and could have said something about her choice of eye shadow, but I was too much of a gentleman, and let it go.

Maybe she forgot who was paying for dinner or giving her a ride home.

Yes, my two front eyeteeth were so prominently out of place, they looked like those plastic fangs you buy at Halloween costume stores.

I always felt self-conscious about my teeth ever since hearing the same comment many times throughout elementary school.

In my teens, I tried to grow a mustache hoping it would camouflage the problem, but it just made me look like a walrus.

People stared at my teeth so much, I would cover my mouth when talking and, sadly, still have that terrible habit to this day.

Even though I was the class clown (no surprise), I was the one who could never smile.

That night's dinner, I realized that I couldn't own this embarrassment for the rest of my life.

Having no other options, I went to see an orthodontist.

After a series of X-rays, not only did he find other crooked teeth, he also discovered that my upper and lower jaws were not aligned properly.

He explained that this was a common condition in people of Irish descent, and referred me to a maxillofacial surgeon.

After a lengthy examination, the surgeon recommended that I first wear braces for a couple of years to straighten my teeth, and then have jaw surgery to bring the top row of teeth forward in alignment with the bottom row.

During this time, I was so good at hiding my teeth that some girls didn't even notice my braces, even while kissing me.

After two years, all my teeth were perfectly straightened and with the braces still on, it was now time for the jaw surgery.

During the five-hour-long operation, the surgeon sliced my top jawbone horizontally and slid it forward to fit my bottom and top teeth together.

Staples were inserted into my upper jawbone to keep it in place while temporary metal wires ran under my cheeks, up through my eye sockets, and back down my jaw, securing the entire front of my face.

Since my teeth and jaw were now wired and locked together, the surgeon gave me a small pair of wire clippers and instructed me on how to use them in case of an emergency, like possibly gagging, which could then result in my choking to death.

Surprisingly, the only pain from the surgery was that of seeing myself in the mirror for the first time.

My face was solidly black and blue, and my cheeks had swelled up to three times their normal size, so my face looked like an abandoned soccer ball at the end of a long season.

I froze and asked myself, "What the hell did I do? Will this ever heal?"

My lips became so chapped after the surgery that for the following few days layers of skin peeled off like a molting snake's skin.

After three days in the intensive care unit, I was transferred to my own room, which happened to have just been freshly painted and decorated.

The paint fumes caused me to have an asthma attack, and the hospital's paramedics had to quickly move me to another room.

When my friends came to visit me in the hospital, they walked into my room, looked at me, and walked out.

The nurse had to guide them back into my room, point at me and say, "There, that's Robert."

The astonishment on their faces was priceless, and worrisome, to say the least.

With my mouth wired shut, eating became my biggest challenge.

My weight dropped from 155 to 115 lbs. in less than a month.

I tried soup, but all the solid ingredients got caught in my braces.

After one spoonful, with my tongue confined behind my teeth, I could only pour the liquid into my mouth rather than slurp it up.

My twenty-dollar blender became my lifeline, mixing food together like hot dogs and chili, or hot milk and cupcakes, to liquefy the concoctions.

All my clothes draped on me, like the poor kid who had to wear his father's old brown suit to go trick-or-treating.

I was so skinny that an old girlfriend stood three feet from me in a store and didn't recognize me, which actually was good because who wants an ex to see you at your worst?

My weight continued to drop so much that my doctor told me that I needed to do something immediately or I'd wind up back in the hospital.

He suggested getting some liquid supplements and protein powder to bulk up like body builders do.

I went to a vitamin store at the local mall and asked the clerk at the cash register if she could help me.

Skinny, swollen-faced, and with teeth wired shut, I mumbled, "I needds zumme liwquid vitaamens an som brotein pouwder."

Her eyes opened wide, and a terrified expression came over her face, like she had just seen the bogeyman.

She said, "Wait here. I'll go check with my manager."

She made her way to the back of the store and had a short conversation with her boss, while pointing in my direction.

After a few minutes of watching them search the shelves, they called me over.

The manager, pretending not to be scared, smiled, and grabbed a large yellow container off one of the shelves before approaching me.

Within inches of my face, she yelled, "THESE ARE VITAMINS, YOU DRINK THEM!" while doing a pantomime of guzzling beer from a large keg.

Obviously, both store personnel concluded that I was either deaf, had some kind of disability, or was from another planet.

Surprised at the volume and intensity of the manager's instructions, I started laughing, but since my teeth were wired shut, I then began to gag and lose my breath.

Now they thought I was having a seizure.

They both shouted at each other on how to save my life.

It was like a classic scene from The Three Stooges, although not at all funny at the time.

One customer saw the commotion and ran to a phone to call 911.

Within minutes, the fire department EMTs flew in through the front door with all their life-saving gear.

After my breathing was brought under control, I soon left the store with a bag full of liquid vitamins and protein powder, on the house!

Long story short, fixing my smile was a lot of work, and cost a lot of money, but getting the braces and surgery was one of the smartest things I ever did and would do again in a heartbeat.

I can now walk into any room and never feel anxious about my smile, or the need to hide my laughter.

On a side note, years later, a girl approached me and said she recognized me because she remembers seeing my photo in my orthodontist's waiting room.

Apparently, I had become the famous "before and after" poster boy, and proud of it!

A SPECIAL CHRISTMAS PARTY

I received a last-minute phone call from a bass player to play drums at an afternoon Christmas party, only he didn't supply many details other than the time and place.

This made me somewhat suspicious because, without much advance information, I have found myself playing with singers who couldn't remember lyrics, guitarists who were constantly out of tune, or band leaders who wrote bad checks.

After blindly agreeing to his invitation, I loaded up my drums and drove to the location, not knowing what to expect but hoping for the best.

Arriving at the address, I soon discovered it was a school for individuals with special needs.

Before I could even park my car, about 20 kids and adults came running towards me like a pack of wild banshees, with many others following close behind in wheelchairs and on crutches.

They opened my car doors, confiscated everything and anything they could grab, and then ran back to the school's large auditorium.

There was so much confusion, all I could do was chase after them in a panic.

As I ran into the hall, I immediately realized that it had been transformed into a winter wonderland of lights and yuletide aromas.

On one wall was a long buffet that had every imaginable platter of entrees, side dishes and desserts, surrounded by twinkling colored lights with a backdrop of a dozen fully-decorated Christmas trees.

At the center of the large room was a huge parquet dance floor with a mirror globe spinning above it.

As it turned out, the bass player who offered me the gig had a sister with special needs, and every year he would hire musicians to play at the school's Christmas party.

All the kids and adults stood around the bandstand waiting and cheering for us to start playing, as if they were about to see a famous rock concert.

Some had on their Sunday's best; the girls donned long formal dresses, while the boys wore second-hand tuxedos with oversized ruffled shirts, and everyone wore tennis shoes!

There were people of all sizes, shapes and colors chanting at us to hurry up and play.

As soon as we started playing, we couldn't help but notice that everyone seemed to know all the lyrics to every song, and they sang along as best they could.

Those who were too shy to come onto the dance floor stood by themselves against the walls, while moving in their own creative wiggles to the music.

Usually, these types of gigs would only last for a few hours, but this audience held us hostage for over seven hours.

Even though we wound up repeating practically every one of our songs, a number of times, there wasn't a single complaint.

By the end of the night, the party looked like one of those dance marathons during the Depression Era where sweaty contestants did everything to stay on their feet by holding each other up and swaying back and forth.

This was the most appreciative audience I can ever remember throughout my musical career, and I continued to volunteer for this gig for years.

THE SHERIFF

As a drummer for over 25 years, playing alongside hundreds of musicians on thousands of gigs, there was always that one life-threatening situation I will never forget.

Back in the 1980s, I joined a very popular band in Los Angeles that played every venue on the Sunset Strip.

One night, at a club called The Central located in West Hollywood, a guitarist from a world-famous blues band happened to be in the audience, and approached us after our set to say he was very impressed with our playing and original music.

His comment seemed a little odd because we actually sounded like a cross between The Doors and Aerosmith, which was the furthest thing away from his style of music.

He proceeded to make us an incredible offer by inviting us to record our first album at his state-of-the-art home studio.

And, for free.

The only catch was that the studio was located on the east coast, and to get there, we had to cover all our own transportation and living expenses.

But, we couldn't pass up this opportunity, so we scraped together all our money and made the trip.

When we arrived at his home located on 20 secluded acres of countryside, we found it impressive to say the least.

After entering through the large, ornamental iron gate, we drove down a long, rambling driveway lined with oak trees that led to a huge, colonial-style mansion at the edge of a beautiful private lake.

We continued past his house to the recording studio.

Then, the entire band settled into a guest cottage in the back.

Our schedule was to record at least 12 hours during the day, and then go out to dinner at night.

It was our last night, and so we decided to visit a popular country bar in the area to check out the local band.

It was like walking onto the set of *Urban Cowboy*.

Tonight's featured band found out we were from Los Angeles, and let us sit in on a number or two, and, by the end of the night, we had brought down the house with some good old rock 'n' roll.

Our handsome lead singer managed to convince a southern belle to come back to the guest house for a drink.

She was a classy petite brunette wearing white sequined cowboy boots that matched her tight-fitting western ensemble.

When we arrived back at the cottage, he immediately took his prize into the bedroom.

Nobody else in the band had any such luck, so the rest of us losers sat in the living room drinking beer and watching TV.

Less than ten minutes later, we could hear some yelling, then bang!

The bedroom door flew open, slamming against a wall.

The cowgirl came running out half naked and headed for the front door.

Moments later, out stepped our lead singer, wearing only his boxer shorts.

"What the hell just happened in there?" I asked.

"That bitch tried to impress me by telling me that her father is the local sheriff who happens to also own the largest gun store in town."

I, for one, slept with one eye open that night, waiting for that hunting rifle to come through the window.

HER BOOK

Have you ever been in a relationship where you would rather risk your own life than get yelled at?

As strange as that may sound, I was in just that kind of relationship.

My girlfriend at the time was an excessive complainer about everything.

She thought she had to educate me on how to buy the correct brand of food, how to eat it, what clothes to wear, when to wear them, and how to read the TV Guide and place it back exactly on the coffee table in such a way so it wouldn't look like anybody read it.

The list goes on.

Yes, it was a living nightmare at times and I often felt like that anxious soldier on patrol who walks in front of army tanks, checking for land mines.

Why would I stay with her?

Well, let's just say she had other qualities that almost made up for it.

At the time, I had a great job in a large factory and if I did my required tasks quickly and with no mistakes, there would be extra free time to read the newspaper, magazines or books.

One day, I decided to borrow my girlfriend's book about my favorite actor, Cary Grant, and bring it to work.

I was at my workstation, contently doing my job when, suddenly, the Whittier Narrows earthquake struck.

The four-story building, constructed of metal girders with high concrete walls, shook and rumbled like an old rusty coffee can full of glass marbles.

Large pipes filled with liquid chemicals and gases that ran throughout the shop began swaying back and forth like Christmas lights in the wind.

People everywhere on the factory floor were yelling, "Earthquake!" as they ran for their lives!

I immediately bolted for the exit, through the maze of endless workstations, running alongside a stampede of gang members, tattooed bikers, and other co-workers.

Tall stacks of boxes rocked back and forth while metal racks of materials emptied onto the floor.

Long rows of florescent lighting bounced up and down, breaking their bulbs and showering glass down upon us like candy from Mexican piñatas.

The whole time I was thinking about what would happen if I became trapped inside this concrete prison.

It would take hours before anyone found me.

What if there was a fire?

I'd be burned alive under some metal girder.

Just as I finally reached the horde of workers in the parking lot outside, it hit me.

In all the excitement, I inadvertently left the Cary Grant book at my workstation.

Even while enduring this extreme trauma, all I could think about was what would be worse; dying in that building or coming home without her book?

The answer was easy.

I immediately turned and ran back against the tide of evacuees, like a desperate salmon swimming upstream against the current.

Co-workers yelled at me to turn around, but I kept going.

The massive dark structure was now echoing the deafening sounds of alarms and sirens.

Huge aftershocks shook the building again and again, knocking me to the ground several times.

Finally reaching my workstation, I saw my worst nightmare and gasped.

Her book had fallen to the floor!

I rushed over to examine it, and, to my relief, there wasn't a scratch on it.

My life has been spared and it felt like I had just experienced a miracle.

I made my way back outside, and a fellow employee ran over and asked, "Are you OK? Why are you smiling? Weren't you scared?"

"I was, but not anymore.

MOTORCYCLES AT NIGHT

We knew every scenic but dangerous mile of Malibu Canyon Road so well that we could drive it in our sleep.

When there was a full moon, the kids in the neighborhood who owned motorcycles would do a 'night run' to the beach.

My first love was a green 1972 Honda CB 500 equipped with side crash bars, a padded sissy bar, and an 8-track player with a set of stereo headphones.

At the time, there were no helmet laws in California, so fully-enclosed headphones would eliminate all the wind noise and allow for a musical backdrop to the wild ride.

On our night runs, there would be at least eight to ten bikers, riding two-abreast through most of the canyons, but on the long straightaways, we would quickly converge into a single line with no more than about ten feet between each rider.

Once we were all in place, the first rider would turn off his headlight, then the second, then the third, etc., until all the headlights were off, which made for a surreal experience.

There was just enough moonlight to see the highway lines, but, God forbid any animal should run into our path.

The death-defying experiment was to see who in the group would be the 'chicken,' and turn on their headlight first.

On one summer night, there were no chickens.

We rode all the way through Malibu Canyon to the beach, then down Pacific Coast Highway to Topanga Canyon, then all the way back home to Chatsworth, with all our lights off.

A total 60-mile ride in the dark.

It was like sitting in the front rocket of an hour-long Space Mountain ride at Disneyland, but without the ticket prices and long lines.

THE GRAPE FARM

One of the major benefits of growing up in the San Fernando Valley during the 1960s were the agricultural areas remaining for kids to explore and play in.

In my neighborhood, it was a five-acre grape farm at the end of our block.

Located on this property was an old wooden two-story farmhouse, a large barn, dozens of small shacks where the grape pickers once lived, and a rusting flat-bed truck that hadn't moved in decades.

Memories of this once glorious working farm were now layered in dirt and cobwebs.

It hosted many rock and grape-throwing fights, as well as the best place to play hide-and-go seek.

The owner of the farm was in his 80s and would only let certain kids onto the property, as he chased the others away with his rusty shovel.

He died on his porch one summer night, and the bugs got to him before the kids found him there the next day.

Rumors soon started about seeing his ghost strolling up and down the rows of grapevines.

From then on, everyone assumed the farm was haunted.

The older kids tried to see who was brave enough to spend the entire night on the farm, but as soon as it got dark, they all grabbed their sleeping bags and ran home.

The layout of the matured rows of large purple grapevines ran at a 45-degree angle to the surrounding streets and, even after the owner died, the grapes continued to grow along with the weeds and rats that took over the property.

Getting bored with throwing the grapes at each other, we decided to target the passing cars on the adjacent street.

We would hide in the grape rows, wait for a car, chuck our handful of grapes, and then run.

After about 20 minutes, we would make sure the coast was clear, and then do it again.

We never got tired of this.

One afternoon, we saw a dilapidated convertible jalopy heading toward us.

The driver seemed so old, he could have been the car's original owner.

We knew he would be an easy target and probably have no chance of catching us.

As this slow-moving quarry came closer, someone shouted the count, "One, two, three!"

We all hurled handfuls of ammunition in unison.

Our victim got totally pelted and lost control of his jalopy, running over the curb and into a telephone pole.

Other drivers stopped to see if he was OK.

He was, except he was completely purple and mad as hell.

We quickly ran down a side alley straight to my parents' garage.

From inside, with the large door propped open about an inch, everyone lay silently on the ground watching to see if anyone was looking for us.

After a few minutes, a parade of half a dozen marked and unmarked police cars slowly circled back and forth through our neighborhood.

We waited at least a half hour, but they didn't go away.

Suddenly, my mom opened the side door, turned on the light and asked, "What the hell are you kids doing?"

Lying quickly, I said, "We're hiding from Little Kevin."

Little Kevin was younger, and a major pest on our block who always tried to hang out with us older kids.

My mom announced, "You kids must be hungry. Come into the kitchen and I'll make lunch."

We all sat around the kitchen table with a buffet of food, eating like little angels.

As my mom was doing the dishes, she looked out the window and said, "Wow, I wonder why there are so many police cars out there? It's lucky you kids are safe in the house."

I don't think she ever knew just how lucky we were.

FINDING MY SLIPPERS

At the age of five, I would often roam through our neighborhood looking for any stray cats or dogs, and bring them home.

If I didn't find any, I would narrow my search by breaking into the neighbors' backyards to continue my quest.

I would keep these critters just long enough until my mom found out, then it became her job to put the animal and me in the car and drive around until we found the house where they came from.

She would tell the owners that somehow their pets must have gotten out, and they needed to fix their gates.

If the owners weren't home, we would just put the animal back in the yard and leave.

Hopefully, it was the right house.

Finally, I got my own pet.

It was a skinny gray-haired cat with white paws that I found sleeping in the alley behind our house.

I appropriately named him Slippers.

Now, thankfully, I would never again need friends or siblings to play with.

In the following weeks, I fed and nurtured him back to a healthy size.

He became my perfect friend, spending the entire day together playing, eating, and napping in the sun.

Slippers was now an indoor cat, but he went outside just to potty and always came back soon after he was done.

He knew he had a great home with humans who loved him, instead of being alone in a dirty alley and exposed to the elements.

I only had him for about six months when one morning I woke up and noticed he wasn't on my bed, which is where he always slept.

No one in my family had any idea where he was or how he possibly got out of the house.

I searched the entire neighborhood and, with help from my mom, put fliers on telephone poles and market bulletin boards, but there was no response.

Heartbroken, I somehow felt it was my fault he got away.

Days later, a neighborhood bully who was just a couple years older than me said, "Hey Bob, I found your cat!"

"Where?"

With a big smile, he said, "Follow me!"

He could run faster than me, but I did my best to keep up.

Every few houses, he would turn back around with a big grin and yell, "Hurry up!"

We finally reached an intersection about two blocks away from home.

The bully laughed as he pointed to the gutter.

There appeared to be a barely recognizable carcass that, apparently, had been run over numerous times.

I stared at Slippers for the longest time, hoping he would wake up, shake off the damage, and come home with me.

In shock, and unable to even cry, I somehow managed to find my way home.

That day, I realized just how cruel people can be.

SANTA SUSANA PASS ROAD

It's hard to believe that my friend, Mikey, and I lived as long as we did, after all the misadventures we were involved in together, but here I am, and still in one piece.

I was cutting my parents' lawn, when Mikey drove up in his dad's old 1964 white 4-door Plymouth with Tommy sitting shotgun.

Two 16-year-olds wearing racing helmets, both without driver's licenses, what are the chances this will turn out well?

We could only assume his dad did not know he borrowed his car for today's adventure.

Their plan was to see how fast Mikey could drive from Chatsworth to Simi Valley on the very winding Santa Susana Pass Road.

The road had been featured in many movies including the 1949 classic, *White Heat*, starring James Cagney, about a gang of robbers in and around the early San Fernando Valley.

It also became the famous road on which Charles Manson's hideout, the Spahn Ranch, was located.

The road is a little over two miles long, with sharp hairpin turns and 300-foot cliffs bordering most all of it.

With no forethought whatsoever, I quickly parked the lawnmower and jumped into the Plymouth's back seat.

Not finding a helmet or seatbelts, I thought, "Why did I get in deathtrap?"

Too late now, as we were already speeding down the street.

As we arrived at the bottom of the pass, Tommy took out his stopwatch to time the event.

Out of nowhere came a small red MG sports car already passing us, honking its horn while the driver waved his hand as to say, "Catch me if you can!"

That was too much for Mikey to handle, so he put the pedal to the metal, and we were off to the races.

With four barrels open, we flew up the mountain, sliding sideways around every corner and, at times, feeling like we were on just two wheels.

Halfway through the canyon, we blew past the MG like it was standing still.

The guts of the old Plymouth roared as we continued our flight up the two-lane road, crossing the double yellow lines on every curve.

Going way too fast, we drifted into the opposing lane just as an old station wagon was coming toward us from the opposite direction.

"We're going to die!" Tommy screamed.

Unable to get back into our lane, we slammed sideways, hitting the oncoming car like we had just qualified for Demolition Derby.

The sound of the impact was deafening.

We knocked the other car nearly over the cliff, leaving it with one spinning rear tire hanging off the edge.

"What should we do?" Mikey yelled.

"Ya gotta go back to see if the other driver is OK," I answered.

Mikey slowed down and reluctantly turned the car around, knowing he could have easily kept going.

We met up with the other driver and found out he was a retired sheriff.

He was shaken up, but laughed about the whole thing.

He said he had seen a lot of this in his career and knew the worst part would be Mikey explaining to his dad what happened to his car.

Mikey exchanged information with him, and we slowly headed home.

Poor Mikey had to come up with a believable story on how one side of his dad's car was completely crushed from bumper to bumper, while it, presumably, sat in the driveway all day.

Although, Mikey could teach a college course in creative storytelling, this time he knew that facing his dad would likely cause more damage than what happened to his car.

REROOFING

I was only 11 years old when my parents uprooted the family from our *Wonder Years* home in Canoga Park, and moved us into a new and much larger house located in Chatsworth, California.

My mom chose this particular home because it was one of the four decorated models that were used to showcase the different options available in the development.

It featured bright red furry carpeting in the living room, olive green cut pile carpeting in the hallways, navy blue carpets in the bedrooms, an oversized foyer with silver and black foil wallpaper, and, to top it off, yellow flower-patterned Formica kitchen counters.

It was the epitome of 1960's pop culture.

It also came with a flat tar roof and a slanted front facade that had a French Colonial style to it.

The house was obviously built in a hurry because, after only a few years, my dad and I were constantly having to climb onto the roof to fix leaks after it rained.

After the 10th year, the front facade became warped from the weather, and small chips of paint littered the driveway.

My dad finally decided that it was time to replace the facade with a different type of building material.

After some research, we agreed that asphalt shingles were our best bet because they would probably last at least 20 more years.

Since neither of us knew how to install shingles, I asked a friend who worked in construction to help us out.

He agreed, quite reluctantly, because it was the middle of summer, and the last thing he wanted was to be up on top of a hot roof all day.

After removing and replacing the old plywood, we tacked down tar paper, and then nailed the asphalt shingles on top.

The sun was setting when we finally finished the job, and my dad was ecstatic about the results.

My friend and I were exhausted, sunburned, and our hands were stained black from handling all the tar and patching material.

He said the only way to properly clean our hands was to douse them in gasoline, dry them with some old rags, and then wash thoroughly using dish soap and water.

I asked my dad if he had any old rags lying around, and he went into the house to look for some.

I grabbed the lawnmower gas can, and we soaked our hands in an old paint bucket.

After a few minutes, our hands were dripping wet and starting to sting from the gasoline.

My dad finally returned with a large cardboard box, and an expression on his face as if he had just found the ultimate treasure trove of old rags.

We were about to shove our wet hands into the box of rags, but noticed they were not your typical household rags.

They were my dad's old tighty-whities that my mom used for dusting, and, apparently, some weren't so white anymore.

My friend looked at me and without skipping a beat he said, "There's no way in hell I'm touching those."

My dad, totally embarrassed, ran back into the house to look for something more user-friendly.

I, on the other hand, didn't even think twice about using those rags to dry my hands.

Someone great once said, "It's not the underwear in your life that counts, it's the life in your underwear."

PULLING THE TRIGGER

One boring afternoon, Kenny, Tim, Doug, and I were sitting around trying to come up with something to do which would not involve damaging property, breaking the law, or fatally injuring someone.

Being only 13 years old, this would be a challenge.

Looking around Kenny's wood-paneled bedroom, I noticed a pair of old rusty rifles mounted on the wall.

"Are those real guns?" I asked.

"They're just old BB guns, but I think they still work."

"Well, there you have it. Let's play a game of war!" I announced.

Without ever giving a minute of thought to our own personal safety, we all agreed and picked teams.

I picked Kenny because he owned the guns and I assumed he was familiar with shooting things, while I, with a great baseball arm, was more qualified at throwing rocks.

The rules were that each two-man team will have one BB gun, and the other weapons would only be either rocks or dirt clods.

We all split up and counted to 100, before engaging the other team.

My mind raced back to all the cowboy and gangster movies I'd seen, and thought about how they would have strategized their attack and defense.

Kenny insisted we crawl up onto the wood-shingled roof of his parents' house to get a better view of the front lawn and backyard, as well as the surrounding neighborhood.

I didn't think it was a good idea because, as we all know, it never works out in the movies because someone always dies falling from a high place.

I spotted the opposing team just on the other side of the neighbor's fence, and saw they had cheated by putting on motocross leathers and helmets.

Too late to worry about it now.

We opened fire and the war began!

Kenny repeatedly shot toward the fence like a whack-a-mole game, as the sound of BBs bounced off their helmets.

Their rocks came close, and some of their BBs did hit us, but we were soldiers now and too busy in combat to think about our injuries.

I raised my head just above the roof line and saw a glass marble launched from a slingshot.

It seemed to be traveling in slow motion, flying across the backyard, hitting the center of my forehead.

The impact propelled me backwards, almost knocking me off the roof.

In the back of my mind, I could hear my mother saying, "It's all fun and games until someone loses an eye!"

And, that someone could have been me.

The other team rushed toward us and vaulted over the fence to get closer, but then retreated to the side neighbor's yard.

Kenny and I decided to trade weapons.

I was now in command of the BB gun.

Tim, from the other team, ducked into some thick bushes and I decided to go after him like I was hunting wild boar.

With the BB gun slung over my shoulder, I slithered down the side of a chimney onto a broken fence, then jumped to the ground.

Creeping around the corner of the house, I made my way through the dense bushes, and then stopped.

I found myself unexpectedly standing over my target, Tim.

He was lying motionless and partly camouflaged by the thick ivy.

He slowly turned his head, looked straight into the barrel of my BB gun, and begged, "Please, please, no, no, don't shoot!"

In those few seconds, I thought to myself do I shoot or show him mercy?

I reflected on the fact that his team had cheated by putting on motocross leathers and helmets.

Thought about the glass marble ricocheting off my forehead.

Thought of the good guys and bad guys in all the westerns and cop movies, and the decisions they had to make.

Thought about what he would do if the circumstances were reversed.

I was done thinking, and quickly pulled the trigger, firing a BB directly into his thigh from about a foot away.

It went through his jeans and the blood started to flow.

He grabbed his leg and howled like a bad actor in a B-horror movie.

We decided the game was over and went back to Kenny's house to assess the damages.

We laid him out on the garage workshop table.

The BB was embedded in Tim's leg.

I suggested giving him a real bullet to bite on during surgery, but the others thought that was another dumb idea.

With some needle-nose pliers, rubbing alcohol, and our amateur surgical skills, we dug down and pulled it out.

Everyone was laughing except Tim — he was still screaming.

At least we didn't get into any trouble that day.

THE SARDINE CAN

Working in a factory for over 20 years, I gained a true appreciation for all types of people from different social and economic backgrounds, and how humor and laughter can bring us all together.

It was an extraordinary learning experience that I will always treasure.

One day, being particularly bored with food in general, I decided to bring in some sardines and crackers for a change in my usual routine of snacking on veggies at work.

It seemed like a good idea at first, but the smell of the oily fish mixed with the distinct aromas of the factory made them extremely unappetizing.

I only ate half the can and wasn't sure what to do with the rest of the sardines.

I didn't want to put them in the trash can in my area because then I would be smelling them for the rest of the day.

Working next to me that day was a woman we called Miss Mary Jane because she smoked so much marijuana, she didn't know where she was half the time.

When Miss Mary Jane went on a bathroom break, I decided to play a joke on her by tucking my half-empty sardine tin behind some supplies, and out of view, at her workstation.

This way, she would be the one to smell the dead fish instead of me.

Upon her return a few minutes later, her face was contorted as if she was smelling something unpleasant.

At first, she starting her armpits, hair, etc.

Then, she casually looked around to see if anyone else noticed the smell, but we all acted like we were very busy doing our jobs.

She walked over to me and asked me, "Honey, do you smell anything weird in my area?"

I walked over to her workstation, took a big whiff, then gave her a strange look, and said, "No."

Meanwhile, all the other workers who had seen what I did were all biting their lips so hard and trying not to laugh that they could barely do their jobs.

After about 15 minutes of checking herself, and every piece of clothing she had on, Miss Mary Jane asked for another bathroom break, presumably, to examine herself even more thoroughly.

While she was gone, I quickly removed the sardine can from her area.

When she came back, surprisingly, the fishy smell was gone.

She probably figured that whatever she did in the bathroom must have eliminated the odor.

I did this hide-and-go-seek with the sardine can about a dozen more times during the day.

By the end of the shift, she confessed to me she would never smoke pot again.

DRIVER SIDE WINDOW

As a drummer in several rock bands during the 1980s, I would frequently get approached by women who not only would ask me out, but also insist that I take their phone numbers.

These numbers were either on business cards, napkins, bar tab receipts, or various other small slips of torn paper.

One girl wanted to write her number on the back of my hand, but I graciously declined because what if she used a permanent marker?

I did not encourage this behavior, and in no way am I bragging, but perks like these come with being a musician.

Not to be impolite to the ladies, I would just thank them and accept their numbers.

Unfortunately, as my luck would have it, I would always get these offers when I was either married, engaged, or had a steady girlfriend, but never when I was single and available.

However, I really didn't want to just throw away these souvenirs.

So, instead, I pathologically started collecting them as trophies, like a serial killer would do.

If only I could find a safe place to stash them because, who knows, I might need them someday?

I wound up dropping them down inside the driver's door window opening in my car.

It was my hidden piggy bank that gave me some abnormal sense of confidence just knowing they were there.

Sure enough, one day, while driving to the store with my girlfriend, I needed to adjust my side-view mirror.

My car didn't have an inside controller, so I had to roll down my window to adjust it manually.

Because of the light rain, as I rolled my window back up, three slips of paper sporting random phone numbers became stuck to the outside of the window.

One of them still had red lipstick on it!

I kept making the window move up and down, trying to knock them off the glass, but they just continued to stick like glue.

My girlfriend began yelling at me, "Shut the freakin' window! It's cold in here,"

But there was no way to do this without her discovering the evidence of my pathetic secret.

The argument heated up and continued until we finally arrived at the store.

When she went inside, I rolled the window completely up, removed all the phone numbers, and threw them in a nearby trash can.

I learned a valuable lesson that day — adjust your mirrors before you drive!

THE GREEK THEATRE

For my 30th birthday, my generous brother surprised me
with front row center seats to a Pat Metheny concert at the
fabulous Greek Theatre, and, if that wasn't enough, he also
rented a black limousine, so we and our girlfriends could
party like celebrities.

The Greek Theatre is located in the foothills above
Hollywood in a beautiful neighborhood surrounded by
multi-million-dollar homes.

On the 45-minute drive to the theater, the beer and
champagne flowed.

As we got closer to the venue, the traffic crawled along at a
snail's pace, if it moved at all.

After all that drinking, I desperately needed to relieve
myself, or I'd explode right in my pants.

The theater was still three or four blocks away, and I knew I
wouldn't make it in time.

There was only one option.

I jumped out of the car and ran up the street about 50 yards,
then ducked into some large bushes by the side of a huge
mansion.

Worried that people in their cars could see me, I leaned in
and answered the call of nature.

I kept looking back over my shoulder to see where our
limousine was, just to make sure it didn't pass me and leave
me behind.

Halfway through my mission, I looked up and straight into a kitchen window.

There stood an elderly lady doing the dishes.

She opened the window and asked, "Who's playing tonight?"

"Pat Metheny, jazz guitarist. Front row center tickets."

"Enjoy yourself."

I smiled and nodded a 'Thank you.'

It was obvious I wasn't the first person to use her million-dollar house as a toilet.

I quickly finished, zipped up, and ran back to the car, which was now exactly in front of her house.

What a relief, and talk about perfect timing.

MALIBU AT NIGHT

I had just parted ways with a girlfriend, or should we say she kicked my ass to the street, and, at the age of 22, the rejection was enough to kill me.

In serious need of a sympathetic shoulder to cry on, I could either pay a shrink $100 an hour to listen to my suffering, or, spend $20 on some cheap beer and spill my guts to a close friend.

I would probably get the same results.

I called my friend Tony because he had a lot of experience with past girlfriends and breakups, and I assumed he would be a good resource.

He was up to the task, and more than happy to oblige since I was buying the beer.

We drove to the nearest liquor store and bought a 12-pack of the cheapest beer they had.

Disappointed by my choice, Tony asked me why the cheap brand, and I explained that talking about my ex-girlfriend didn't deserve the expensive stuff.

Somehow, that made sense to me at the time.

We headed back to my parents' garage to do some serious soul searching.

We stopped at a traffic light where, coincidentally, two girls pulled up next to us.

They smiled at Tony, and he smiled back.

At the next light, one of the girls yelled out, "Hey where are you guys going?"

From ten feet away, they both appeared to be our age, seemed to have all their teeth, and were attractive enough for an intersection conversation.

Tony yelled back, "We're going to the beach to have a couple of beers."

Both girls looked at each other, hesitated for a moment, and then the driver asked, "Can we join you?"

Still upset in my condition, the very last thing I wanted to do was meet another girl, but Tony insisted.

He yelled back, "Sure, follow us!"

They did — the entire 25 miles to Malibu beach.

All the way there, I confessed out depressed I felt about the breakup.

We all parked along Highway 1 near the pier.

Hiking down to the sand, we introduced ourselves and made small talk.

We found an ideal retreat out of view from the highway, and commenced handing out the beers.

Now I wished I had bought the more expensive brand because these made me look like a big cheapskate.

Between the blanket of stars and the calm cobalt ocean, it was postcard perfect and the sand was still warm from the day.

A handful of surfers were still scattered among the fluorescent waves, waiting, unsuccessfully, for their ride to take them in.

We all chatted for about fifteen minutes until Tony paired up with the brunette to take a long, quiet stroll down the beach.

I guess they were anxious to see if they had anything in common.

Left with the blonde, we both continued to watch the last surfer paddle in.

She was a quintessential California girl, with tanned skin, sun-streaked hair, green eyes, and a trusting smile you only see in toothpaste ads.

Her lavender sweater fitted as tightly as her faded jeans.

The fragrance of a girl's perfume mixed in with the cool ocean breeze induced me to think I had died and gone to heaven.

If this was the road to recovery, I'm all in.

Only one day after my breakup, the love gods had smiled down on me.

We continued our conversation about where we lived, went to school, and what we wanted to do in life.

As we talked, she began moving closer.

And then closer.

Since I had just met her an hour ago in traffic, I could only assume that, at this point, she had good intentions.

She slowly, but assertively, leaned in towards me.

I closed my eyes with anticipation while thinking, "Is this really happening?"

Just as our lips almost touched, I heard a loud voice say, "Let's go!"

I opened my eyes to see Tony with the other girl standing over us.

Tony's face and chest were covered with fresh vomit, and you could tell what someone had for dinner.

My new friend sprang up and apologetically said, "Sorry."

The girls ran back to their car and screeched the tires as they left.

I asked Tony what happened.

He just mumbled something about his new acrobatic approach to kissing.

Apparently, that night I wasn't the only one spilling my guts.

TOPANGA CANYON

You couldn't have asked for a more picture-perfect day to own a motorcycle and cruise to Malibu for the afternoon.

I asked my friend, Kenny, to come along, and sat him behind me on my beautiful green 1973 Honda CB 500.

I only had this bike for less than a year, but probably waxed it more than a dozen times.

It looked better than brand-new and was my pride and joy.

We started our adventure through the Santa Monica mountains by way of the winding and picturesque Topanga Canyon Road.

Arriving at the coast, we navigated up Highway 1 for about a mile to Topanga Beach, and parked next to a group of motorcycles.

As we walked towards the edge of the cliff that overlooked the ocean, the other bikers invited us to join them and graciously offered us some beer.

With the ocean breeze, endless views of bikinis and an ice-cold beer, it doesn't get any better than that.

Sitting with the other bikers, I happened to reach into my pocket and found a marijuana cigarette.

I couldn't remember how it got in my possession because I never bought the stuff or even smoked that often because of my asthma.

At the time, marijuana was still illegal, and I wasn't really into sharing my stash with people I didn't know, but since they gave us some beer, I returned the favor.

I lit the joint and passed it down the row of the eight other bikers and their girlfriends.

It went down and never came back, so that was the end of that.

About ten minutes later, a girl frantically stood up and said, "Hey, what kind of pot was that? I'm really freakin' high!"

Being a smart ass, I jokingly said, "It's just regular pot, but I sprayed it with Raid to kill the roaches."

I thought that was funny because of the pun on "roach."

Apparently, she didn't get the joke.

She started yelling that I tried to poison her.

Being high myself, all I could do was laugh, which made her freak out even more.

Everyone else stayed calm and continued to enjoy the view.

About an hour later, Kenny and I thought our buzz had worn off enough, and we decided to head home.

We said our goodbyes and rode back through Topanga Canyon towards the San Fernando Valley.

Everything was going fine when I noticed some white smoke coming from the back tires of the car in front of us.

I thought to myself, 'Smoke, why on earth would smoke be coming from the back tires?'

I was unable to put two and two together fast enough to realize that the smoke was coming from the skidding tires.

I applied my brakes but couldn't stop in time.

Slamming into the back of the car, I was catapulted over the handlebars, onto the trunk and rear window glass, then ricocheted and tumbled into oncoming traffic like a black and orange crash dummy.

An oncoming car stopped inches from my head, which could have been fatal as there were no helmet laws back then and I'd never worn one.

I looked back at my bike and saw Kenny doubled up on top of the gas tank in a daze.

The woman driver jumped out of her car and started crying because she wasn't paying attention either, when she unexpectedly slammed on her brakes.

The reason she said she stopped so suddenly was because another car had cut her off while turning into a nudist colony.

She apologized profusely and offered money for any damages, but I refused.

We noticed that I had cracked her rear window, but she said not to worry about it.

I was badly scraped up with a lot of bleeding, but nothing seemed to be broken.

Traffic was backing up and I heard an ambulance siren in the distance.

Not wanting to make a big deal out of the whole incident, I just wanted to get the hell out of there before the highway patrol showed up.

With numerous scars from that accident, and many others like it, I did eventually sell my motorcycle.

My only regret is that I never did find that nudist colony.

HIGH SCHOOL TRACK MEET

My mother often experimented with exotic foods and recipes, which meant there was always a culinary surprise awaiting us at mealtimes.

We were once served a big bowl of blue Jell-O with frozen fish sticks floating inside.

She called this savory dish, "Her Breaded Mermaids."

If we were scared and refused to eat what she brought to the table, my dad would intervene, and with utter intention say, "Eat it or wear it."

This meant we had no choice in the matter.

In the long run, we gained a broader appreciation of various cuisines and foods from around the world, and her imagination.

One day, she came home from the supermarket with a six-pack of lunchbox-sized pineapple juice cans, and she told us about their wonderful high vitamin C content and other nutritional benefits.

The juice tasted bitter at first, nothing like my vision of beautiful pineapple trees swaying in the wind on some tropical island.

Maybe if I drank more, it could be the turning point in my life that was currently filled with the over-consumption of caffeinated soft drinks.

After trying for a couple of weeks, the taste became more palatable, and I was drinking at least a can or two a day.

I decided to share the yummy drink with my fellow track team members at one of our critical competitions.

We were on the field getting ready before the opposing team was to show up, and I pulled out a couple of dozen cans from my gym bag, which had been sitting in the hot sun for most of the day.

I explained to my teammates how special the juice was, and how it would give them the extra energy needed to win.

Then I distributed cans to everyone like a medical charlatan selling snake oil from the back of a covered wagon.

My teammates gathered around me, each grabbing a can or two and eagerly downing them as fast as they could.

Within a half hour, it appeared as if the pineapple juice did not quite agree with everyone.

One kid barfed all over our team captain while they sat together in the bleachers.

The captain jumped up, and stuck out his chest like a rooster, in a futile attempt to prevent the kid's lunch from dripping down his back.

Another kid had such bad stomach cramps that he curled up in a ball and was unable to move off the track field.

He kept yelling for his mommy while three teammates dragged him a hundred yards into the locker room like a dead horse.

Not surprisingly, it was our worst track meet of the year, and a bitter reminder every time a see a pineapple.

HOW I LEARNED TO DROWN

One of my earliest memories was when I was only five or six years old, and a neighborhood bully tried to kill me.

Fortunately, he failed.

He knew I couldn't swim, but he proceeded to coax me into the deep end of a swimming pool, and then told me to push off downwards.

I did, and sank helplessly to the center of a nightmare.

Though desperately trying to grab onto anything or anybody for help, I soon blacked out.

The next memory was opening my eyes and finding myself on the hot pool deck surrounded by people taking turns administering CPR, and hearing the diminishing sound of an ambulance siren as it was pulling up.

After that horrifying experience, I knew I could never go near a body of water again.

However, at the age of nine, my parents, having grown tired of dealing with my debilitating fear of water, took me to the local park for swim lessons.

They encouraged me to at least give it a try.

On the first lesson, the coach instructed all the kids to line up at the shallow end, then jump in and quickly turn around to hold on to the edge of the pool.

As simple as that sounded, when I heard "Jump," I panicked and ran out of the pool yard crying.

Then, at age 13, I was preparing for my confirmation at St. Mel Catholic Church in Woodland Hills.

During my religious classes, my mom waited for me in the church's parking lot where she befriended an elderly couple who lived in the apartment building next door.

They soon became my adopted grandparents, and would invite my mom and me over for homemade treats after my classes.

Their building complex featured a large swimming pool in the center courtyard, and, of course, I was terrified to even walk around it on the way to their apartment.

I would hug the walls of the building, with my back to the pool, keeping my eyes looking straight up and never behind me.

The old gentleman heard about my phobia and offered to teach me how to swim.

I kept politely declining, but he kept adamantly insisting.

He was a big guy who had been a lifeguard in college, and at the public beaches.

I reluctantly agreed to his offer, and brought my swim trunks the following week.

Together, we slowly entered the warm pool, him with his half-smoked cigarette dangling from his mouth with a tapeworm of ashes still attached, and me with my all-consuming fears.

He began telling me stories, like how he started a beer brewing company in Los Angeles, and owned a 1,000-plus acre ranch in Malibu, only to lose everything during the Great Depression.

In between each colorful story, he gave me instructions on how to swim and stay afloat.

Before I knew it, I was doing laps and completely submerging my head under water.

Over the following weeks, I continued to take advantage of his pool and his lessons.

For my confirmation gift, my adopted grandparents gave me a large, square-shaped St. Christopher medal to wear around my neck on a long chain.

They said it would always protect me and bring me good luck.

At that time, my dad worked as an engineer at Rocketdyne in the San Fernando Valley, and one of the perks of his job was access to an employee recreation park that had two swimming pools.

The shallow pool was mostly for mothers and their toddlers who, consequently, often turned the water yellow by the end of the day.

The larger ten-foot-deep pool had a diving board, where I learned to do jackknives and flips.

Feeling confident in my newfound swimming abilities, I decided to dive to the bottom of the deeper pool and explore the shiny chrome drain cover.

While checking out the drain, my St. Christopher medal slipped through the grids of the cover and become entangled.

I kept tugging and tugging, but was trapped.

Finally, and totally out of air, all my nightmares came flooding back.

I pulled as hard as I could, breaking the chain, and then raced to the water's surface.

Lying on the side of the pool, I remembered what the old man once told me: "Always face your fears. You have nothing to lose."

Days later, I did just that and climbed back into that pool and, eventually, even went on to excel at water skiing, high diving, surfing, and other water sports.

The old man was right, I had nothing to lose except my fears.

THE RAIN

I was rehearsing with a band in a studio near the corner of Sunset and Gower in Hollywood, when a guitar player from another band across the hall approached me and said they needed a drummer for their band.

He said he was really impressed with my solid timing and how I creatively applied the entire drum set into the songs.

He wanted me to audition sometime soon and asked for my phone number.

A few weeks later, he called and asked me to come back to Hollywood for that promised audition.

It was cold and rainy that night, and my truck didn't have a shell on the back to protect my drums, so my brother offered to drive me and my gear in his car.

We drove in circles around Hollywood in the pouring rain trying to find the rehearsal location, and eventually located it on a small side street.

It was an old building covered in graffiti, with homeless people hanging around the outside, along with what looked like drug addicts in search of their next fix.

I approached the building, opened the large front door, and was smacked in the face with the odor of putrid stench.

It felt like I had just inhaled a gas station bathroom's tile floor.

I entered a long, dark hallway strewn with people either sleeping or passed out on the floor, and behind several closed doors blared the sounds of half a dozen bands, all playing at the same time like a distorted pinball arcade.

I quickly sized up the situation and decided it wasn't a safe place to unload my drums, and probably not worth the bother to do so.

We then drove to a nearby phone booth to call and leave a message that I had car trouble and couldn't make it.

They never called back.

Months later, while eating my Top Ramen and watching either *American Bandstand* or *MTV,* a new and upcoming band that just hit the charts was introduced on the show.

Oh, my God!

It was the very band that had asked me to audition.

What a fool I was for passing up one of the best opportunities that could have ever come my way.

They were one of the greatest bands that came out of the 1980s, and are still one of my favorites.

From that moment on, I have never turned down any audition, no matter what my first, second, or third impression might be.

As they say, you can never judge a book by its cover, or in my case, know what's on the other side of a door.

SUICIDE HOTLINE

I was extremely proud of my first apartment, which featured a hand-carved waterbed frame, a three-tiered cinder block bookcase, an assortment of large indoor palm trees, a brand new refrigerator, and my very own answering machine.

As a musician, it was essential to own an answering machine, since there were no cell phones back then.

For the young people out there who don't know what an answering machine is, I'll explain.

It is a stand-alone, electronic device that needs to be plugged into a land-line telephone jack, and records incoming voice messages on a cassette tape throughout the day when you weren't home.

These machines didn't have the technology to keep track of or identify the individual callers or their phone numbers, so unless they left their names or messages, you had no idea who called.

Sometimes, I would come home to find dozens of hang-ups or empty messages from the day, not knowing who they were from.

However, just like the cell phones of today, one nice feature of these answering machines was that you could record any outgoing message for the caller to hear.

Example, "At the sound of the tone, please leave your name and phone number, and I'll get back to you."

To reduce the number of hang-ups, I needed to change my outgoing message in order to motivate the callers to at least say something.

I tried a lot of different messages like, "Please, please I beg you…" or "I'll give you a dollar if you…," but nothing was really working.

I eventually created a message that was soul searching and very personal, that would inspire people to respond before hanging up.

My outgoing message was this: "Thank you for calling the Valley Suicide Hotline. At the sound of the tone, please leave your name, number, and how, when, and why you want to end it all, and we'll try to get back to you. Hopefully, before it's too late."

Well, that seemed to solve the problem.

I never had a hang-up again!

Not to make light of the act of committing suicide, but people couldn't wait to be creative about how they would commit suicide, as if it was a common underlying idea they had at one time or another.

Try it and see.

Not the suicide part, but the outgoing message.

THE JUMP CLUB

Every neighborhood has the daredevils, the showoffs, and the kids that always took everything they did to the next level.

Whether it was destroying every car their parents owned, or turning an innocent summer block party into a life-or-death contest.

We were driven by the empty-headed reasoning that today was going to be our last day on earth, with no regard for tomorrow.

If you were living in the San Fernando Valley, California during the 1970s, and you went to a house party hosted by teenagers, it would be just like in the movies, *Animal House* or *Sixteen Candles*, if not more so.

Kids were crammed into every room, closet, and, sometimes, even on rooftops.

Standard ingredients for a successful party; blaring music, alcohol, drugs, under-aged kids, and, of course, no adult supervision.

One hot summer night, as the party was at a fever pitch, my good friend, Mikey, and I felt the need to entertain the raging crowd.

We went into the kitchen and grabbed a couple of long butcher knives and cans of beer, and then went to his parents' bedroom upstairs.

(Why we grabbed butcher knives, I'll never know.)

We climbed out his parents' bedroom window, carefully crawled around the wood-shingled roof, then back up and around to the highest point on the house, dressed in just our boxer shorts.

Some of the loose wooden shingles slid down onto the crowd standing around the swimming pool below, which got everyone's attention.

Our half-witted plan was to run down the ten feet of sloped roof; then clear the first-floor kitchen roof, then three feet of cement pool decking and, hopefully, land safely in the pool.

Mikey and I looked at each other while holding our beers and long butcher knives, nodded, and like in the scene from *Butch Cassidy and the Sundance Kid*, ran down the roof and jumped.

"Let's party!" we yelled.

The audience of party guests erupted in applause and cheers.

We splashed down in the center of the deep end.

I went again but, this time, I wanted to up the game, and so I decided to do a front flip into the pool because, if I was going to die, I might as well do it in style.

Another perfect landing.

Some guy from the party tried to do the same, but because he didn't think he had to run that fast to land in the pool, soon found out he was wrong and scraped half the skin off his back on the pool decking.

The pool got so red from his blood that everyone quickly climbed out.

Years later, I had forgotten all about this crazy night of stunts until someone described the entire episode on Facebook. "Does anyone remember seeing two guys at a party jumping from a roof with butcher knives into a pool?"

I guess we made a bigger splash than I thought.

THE CHRISTMAS GIFT

My family had a tradition when it came to buying Christmas gifts for each other.

They didn't have to be expensive, but they did have to be very personal and thoughtful.

I was always so good at finding the perfect gift that my recipient would say, "How did you know I wanted this?"

It was Christmas Eve, and while wrapping all my presents, I discovered that I had forgotten to buy a gift for my mom.

Oh my God, the one person in my life I really wanted to remember at Christmas.

It was already 8:30 p.m., and so I didn't have very many options.

Should I make something for her?

No.

I was ten, and too grown-up to do that.

The only solution was to find something at the local drugstore that might, hopefully, still be open.

I quickly dressed and ran the three blocks in the freezing cold.

As I flew in the door, I could hear over the intercom, "The store will be closing in five minutes. Please bring all your items to the checkout counter now."

I raced up and down every aisle, but nothing looked good enough for my mom.

The last aisle was the cosmetics and jewelry section.

Again, over the intercom, "The store is closing in one minute."

Just then, I saw in the jewelry case a bracelet and matching clip-on earrings with large fake diamonds, something Auntie Mame would wear on stage.

The manager came over and with folded arms said, "Sorry, the store is closed and you'll have to leave."

"I can't go home without buying these for my mom!"

Some of the fluorescent store lights were being turned off as I pleaded my case.

The manager stared down at me, then went behind the counter, grabbed the jewelry, and said, "OK, let's hurry!"

We quickly made our way to the cash register at the front of the store.

By then, most all the lights were out.

He rang up the jewelry and said, "That will be $12.98."

I searched my pockets twice and discovered that in my rush to leave the house, I had forgotten my money.

He mercifully looked down at me and, after a long pause, smiled and said, "Come back after Christmas and pay for them."

I ran home and snuck in through the kitchen door while everyone was still watching TV.

As I wrapped the present, I now regretted buying it.

Everyone is going to know the diamonds and silver are fake and I'm going to look like an idiot.

I slipped the present behind all the others, so maybe it would be the last one opened after everybody left.

The next morning, the family gathered around the Christmas tree and started taking turns opening their presents.

My sister and brothers loved the presents I got for them.

While collecting all the discarded wrapping paper, my sister found my mom's present behind the tree and said, "Mom, here's the last present. It's from Bobby."

My stomach knotted up with anxiety as my mom slowly unwrapped the small box.

She just stared down at my gift of cheap costume jewelry, and said nothing for what felt like forever.

Then, with a huge smile, she said, "Oh my God. These are absolutely beautiful. Just what I wanted!"

My mother turned my nightmare into a loving memory as only she could.

THE BIG CALM

My dream was to be the world's greatest drummer, or at least die trying.

Which I almost did.

I quickly found that it takes real money to buy music gear, in addition to all the other necessities to living on one's own.

Unfortunately, I had to take a day job in a large factory to make ends meet.

Some days, I would be soldering lead parts while wearing a fully-enclosed protective body suit, or unloading parts off a train's boxcar that were so heavy that, by the end of the day, my knuckles would drag on the ground like a gorilla's.

All this was very physically demanding and the furthest thing from being a drummer, but no matter how good of a player you are, paying gigs were few and far between.

If you ask any successful musician or entertainer, they will tell you that luck played the most important part in their careers.

My 20-hour day consisted of starting in the factory at 6 a.m., working a nine-hour shift before rushing home to pack up my drums and race to either a gig or a rehearsal with one of the many bands I was in, and then taking college courses with any free time I had.

On top of all that, I was going through a breakup with a girlfriend, which was extremely emotional and draining.

One afternoon, while working the morning shift at the factory, my heart felt like it was exploding out of my chest.

I dropped to my knees.

My foreman rushed me to the factory's small, on-site medical center.

After a quick examination, the nurse didn't think anything was too serious, but, just to be cautious, she instructed me to go see a cardiologist that afternoon.

At the doctor's office, he listened to my chest, asked me a lot of questions, and made me run on a treadmill while hooked up to a dozen wires connected to some electrical device.

He, also, didn't seem too concerned at the time, and said to come back the following day for my test results.

I thought nothing of it and assumed it may simply have been heartburn.

When I came back to the cardiologist's office the next day, the receptionist said, "The doctor is next door at the hospital and he'll meet you in the lobby."

I figured he was busy doing his morning rounds and walked over to see him.

In the hospital's lobby stood the doctor and a nurse with a wheelchair.

He quickly informed me that I could have a massive heart attack at any moment and needed to get to the intensive care unit as soon as possible.

After hearing that, I almost did.

The nurse sat me in the wheelchair and quickly rolled me down a long hallway to the intensive care unit.

Sheer panic came over me, knowing my life could be over in seconds.

While asking me for names and phone numbers of my next of kin, they helped me into a bed and hooked me up to an electrocardiogram machine.

After watching the zigzag line move up and down for a few minutes, I politely asked the nurse to turn the heart monitor the other way, so I didn't have to witness myself flatline.

I looked around the room and saw a woman standing by a bed with her arms around two kids who were too young to understand what they were watching.

There lie a motionless body, as a priest was making the sign of the cross and mumbling some words.

On the other side of the room was a woman attached to a set of jumper cables.

Doctors and nurses tried to jolt her back to life but, after 20 minutes, they shook their heads and finally gave up.

This ICU seemed to be a busy mortuary, and I was beginning to think this room was a bit unlucky, with two down and one to go.

I started to shiver and felt myself mentally losing control but then, suddenly, I felt nothing.

Is this the end?

A sense of peace took over as I lay there motionless.

Thoughts of not working nine-hour days in the factory, playing late night gigs into all hours of the night, and no more failed relationships.

No more struggles or disappointments.

That night, a variety of family and close friends came by to visit.

Some of them I hadn't seen in years.

I guess they felt guilty and needed to pay their last respects.

After two days in the hospital and more tests, my cardiologist determined that I was not going to have a heart attack but had just developed a bad heart murmur.

He gave me a medical card to keep in my wallet, explaining the odd rhythm of my heart.

That week, I learned that life can be taken away at any moment, and I should appreciate what little time we have.

I didn't slow down, but continued my busy schedule, and even more so because I'm not going to wait for the end.

It'll have to catch me.

www.ingramcontent.com/pod-product-compliance
Lightning Source LLC
Chambersburg PA
CBHW060501130626
46553CB00002B/384